Living
with
the
Animals

Charles Birch &
Lukas Vischer

Living
with
the The Community
of God's
Creatures
Animals

Risk
BOOK SERIES

WCC Publications, Geneva

Cover design: Rob Lucas
Cover illustration: Detail from "Der Garten der Lüste",
Hieronymus Bosch

ISBN 2-8254-1227-9

© 1997 WCC Publications, World Council of Churches,
150 route de Ferney, 1211 Geneva 2, Switzerland

No. 77 in the Risk Book Series

Printed in Switzerland

Table of Contents

Foreword

How can a system that protects Madonna's royalties by imposing trade barriers against pirated productions of her music not also protect the rights of indigenous peoples?

That question was recently raised in a critique of the priorities of the World Trade Organization. Behind it lies the struggle of indigenous peoples around the world who are seeking to defend their lands and livelihoods against the pollution and destruction caused by mining and logging. Through their actions, they are not only protecting themselves and their own cultures, but also saving numerous species living on the land.

Indigenous peoples are well aware of the web of life of which they are a part and on which they depend. Their claim for justice and life in dignity includes a call for the protection of creation. And so they reject both environmentalists who ignore the quest for justice and developmentalists who are blind to the consequences of economic growth.

Do not separate what belongs together. The culture or civilization that does not take into account its own destructive impact on creation, the suffering it causes to human beings and other forms of life, will finally destroy its own basis. It has no future. At the same time it constantly betrays and makes impossible the praise of God the Creator. This is the scandal which challenges Christians to commit themselves to struggle for justice, peace and creation.

It was Charles Birch whose remarkable speech at the fifth assembly of the World Council of Churches in Nairobi in 1975 opened the eyes of many in the ecumenical movement to acknowledge and take up their responsibility for creation. As a world-renowned scholar of biology, he has contributed much to the debate on sustainability. And he has always questioned a romanticizing understanding of the integrity of creation.

Lukas Vischer, who served the WCC for many years as director of Faith and Order, has in recent years put much of his energy and expertise at the disposal of the WCC's work on climate change. In the 1980s he was also a driving force behind the discussion on "The Rights of Nature" in the World Alliance of Reformed Churches.

In this book, these two experienced ecumenical leaders join forces to offer a stimulating contribution on a related subject which is emerging with new importance in the light of the realities of contemporary civilization: the relationship between human beings and animals.

It should not be taken for granted that Christians and the churches already have sufficient ethical sensitivity to address the issues at stake here: an intriguing survey whose results were published recently was conducted by Harold Takooshian, a sociologist at Fordham University. His research disclosed that in the debate on animal experimentation — one of the topics treated in this book — the groups that gave the lowest rating to animals and the highest level of approval to vivisection were farmers, hunters and the clergy!

Martin Robra
Executive Secretary
Programme Unit on Justice, Peace and Creation
World Council of Churches

Introduction

What is our relationship with animals? What does it mean to share the same planet with them? This question, which has always been asked by human beings, is posed in a different way today. The relationship between humanity and animals has undergone a fundamental change in the context of technological civilization. Human beings have extended their environment to the disadvantage of animals. As never before, animals are dominated by humans and subject to their arbitrary decisions.

On the one hand, people do not have to depend on animals so obviously as in times past. Their aid is no longer essential in many areas of human life. In transportation and agriculture, for example, motors have taken over many operations once carried out by animals. Oddly enough, "horsepower" remains the current term of measurement, although real horses no longer have any part in these functions. As the technical devices made by human beings do the necessary work, animals vanish from the field of human awareness.

On the other hand, the technical supremacy which humans have won by their own efforts leads to an invasion of the living space of animals. To feed themselves, human beings take over animal territory for agriculture and industrial production. The habitats of undomesticated animals too are increasingly restricted. Hunting and fishing are now so efficient as to deprive animals of even a sporting chance, and wild animals, once a threat to humans, are now largely under their control.

Consequently, human aggression against animals has intensified dramatically. The issue is no longer the slaughter of individual animals but the extinction of entire species. Admittedly, animal species have always become extinct. Nature has a history. Every species has its own time and will come to an end sooner or later. The existence of the human race, too, is finite. But the process currently unfolding is especially alarming because it is so rapid and unremitting, and above all because its source is our own behaviour. Entire species of plants and animals are vanishing because the demands of the human species have destroyed their essential conditions of life.

That does not mean that people of our generation are no longer really aware of animals. Indeed, they find them just as fascinating as ever. Research into animal life has never been so intensive. Scientific work in this field is very popular. Animal books and films sell in vast quantities. The number of domestic animals — from dogs and cats to guinea pigs and goldfish — is constantly rising. They are essential "pets" and "companions", not just for children and lonely adults, but for many others too.

Animals have always had a profoundly significant place in the human imagination in ways that have nothing to do with their actual existence as this or that animal. It is as if people see something of themselves and their own lives reflected in these creatures and their behaviour. In the world of allegory, fable and fairy-tale, animals serve as keys to human existence. They are given human characteristics and introduce people to worlds which they could never otherwise enter. They appear as symbolic figures in our dreams. Animals have something approaching a "second existence" in the human mind and fantasy. Children come to know animals in books and cartoons and stuffed toys before they meet them as living creatures, and their acquaintance with these animal "characters" bears no relation to the living creatures they represent. An immense gulf separates the animals inhabiting the human psyche from those in the real world; indeed, these anthropomorphic figures can even block access to real animals. It is interesting to consider from this standpoint the use of animal imagery and caricatures in modern advertising, which turns animals into bearers of human messages.

Unfortunately, all of this has not halted but hastened the destruction of animals in the real world. It does seem, however, that people are becoming increasingly uneasy about the extent of the devastation. As if to limit the results of this process, animal protection has developed in the context of technological civilization, partly on the basis of

Christian motivation. It is an attempt to protect the living space of animals from human exploitation and violence. The movement was ridiculed at first, but over the course of time has gained growing recognition and has successfully established a number of principles and legal measures to help animals. The constant mounting of new campaigns reminds our society that animals have their own dignity and therefore rights of a certain kind.

Above all, it is the disappearance of whole species which has led to new initiatives in this area. Alarm at the destructive role of human beings in creation is beginning to spread. The call to maintain the great variety of species is heard on all sides. Measures to protect threatened species — seals, whales and elephants — are now being pursued seriously. Already it is no longer acceptable to wear "garments of skin" (Gen. 3:21), at any rate if the skins come from rare animals. The most important step has been taken at the level of the United Nations: the adoption at the Earth Summit in Rio de Janeiro in 1992 of a convention on biodiversity, that is, the maintenance of the variety of species on this planet.

Yet the effect of all these measures has been limited. Animal protection is no more than a corrective manoeuvre. There is no guarantee that the convention on biodiversity will lead to a major reversal of relations between humans and animals. To date, the general orientation of technological society has remained unchanged. It is still a fact that the relationship between the human and animal worlds is out of kilter and that the work of destruction continues unabated.

What are the implications of all this? Can humankind go on extending its territory in this way? Can it continue its onslaught on the great variety of animal species — which God made "of every kind" — with impunity? Surely such behaviour represents a fundamental challenge to God's covenant "with every living creature". Does this cruelly destructive process not betray something of the fatal degeneracy of our present way of life? And surely our arbitrary treatment of

God's creation will eventually turn on us. In one sense, indeed, every vanishing species is an intimation of the end of the human race.

Against this background, what does it mean to speak of our responsibility to animals? What can we glean from Scripture in this respect?

Part One:
Lessons from the Bible

Lukas Vischer

1. The Community of the Sixth Day of Creation

The testimony of the Bible sees humans and animals in close community. They are near to one another. Even though the special role of human beings is emphasized, Scripture as a whole takes it for granted that animals form part of the human environment.

To many this statement may sound surprising. The assertion that the Judaeo-Christian tradition not only puts human beings at the centre of creation but also makes all creatures subject to them often goes unchallenged. On this view, the extra-human species represent the "beastly" level, to which humankind must not sink. But there is no warrant for this in the language of the Bible itself. It sees animals in proximity to humans and as part of their immediate environment. They are God's creatures, and like all that he has made they are bound to praise him. The degradation of animals to the status of objects finds no justification in the Bible. While the cultural roots of it are in antiquity, it is essentially the product of the sequence of modern thought since Descartes (1596-1650), which has made humankind the centre of the universe and has seen the outside world as subject to the human mind.

In Part V of his *Discourse on Method*, Descartes describes animals as *automates* (automata). There is no underlying contempt here; rather, Descartes's desire to stress the uniqueness of human beings forces him to such a conclusion. In his view, the rational minds of human beings distinguish them from animals. Bodies are machines made by God:

> Those who know how many automata and moving machines human industry can produce with minimal means, compared with the vast number of bones, muscles, nerves, arteries, veins and all the other parts to be found in the body of every animal, will see this body as a machine which, because it is made by the hands of God, is incomparably better designed than any product of human invention.

Rational beings, however, are more than machines. Even if it proved possible to produce machines that were indistinguishable from animals, we could never produce a machine "that would act in all the circumstances of life just as our reason makes us act". Animals do not possess reason. Descartes is categorical about this: "It is not that animals have less reason than humans; they have none at all." The rational mind cannot be developed from matter. It must be expressly created by God. "The soul must be united with the body to constitute a true human being." Descartes firmly rejects the view that "the animal soul is of the same nature as ours, and that accordingly, like flies and ants, we have nothing to fear or hope for after this life... Our soul is wholly independent of the body... It is immortal."

The primary objective of these statements by Descartes is to assure us of "the existence of God and of the soul". But their inevitable consequence is a clear contradistinction between humans and animals. The rational soul of human beings assigns them to a different world. They are infinitely superior to animals, which are all but reduced to the status of artefacts.

This is not the testimony of the biblical tradition. Scripture bears witness that humans and animals form one community. According to the creation story in Genesis 1, God created humans and animals on one and the same day. The six days of creation correspond to one another. On the first three days the spaces are created, on the fourth, fifth and sixth days creatures come into existence to fill the space. On the second day the waters below the sky are separated from those above the sky, and the oceans are created. Correspondingly, on the fifth day the water and air are filled with fish and birds. On the third day, God causes the "dry land" — that is, the earth — to appear out of the waters and to put forth vegetation. This corresponds to the sixth day, on which God summons animals and humans, the population of the earth, into existence. The common destiny of animals and humankind could hardly be underlined more emphatically.

The second creation narrative in Genesis 2 has similar accents. God creates the cattle, the birds of the air and the animals of the field as "helpers" of humanity. Adam is invited to see what he will call them. "And whatever he called every living creature, that was its name" (Gen. 2:19). By naming the animals, humans enter into a special relationship with them. They are not asked to name *everything* God has made. The task is limited to the animals. A special bond unites humans and animals, because God has designated them as helpers of humankind. Each animal received its name from humankind. Whatever humans called it, "that was its name". In this way humans and animals were joined in an indissoluble community. To be sure, this community is incomplete. It is one-sided, for animals can respond to human beings only to a limited extent. True community comes into being for Adam only when he sees Eve as "bone of *my* bones and flesh of *my* flesh" (Gen. 2:23). Genuine, full and entirely reciprocal community can exist only between human beings. But this does not mean that human beings and animals as God's creatures could not also be related to one another as a community.

This community of creatures is the background against which Scripture emphasizes the special position of humans within creation. God distinguishes humans from animals by making them capable of a special relationship with the Creator. To be sure, God blessed the fish of the sea and the birds of the air as well as humans. But it is not the same blessing. Whereas in the case of the other creatures we are told that God blessed them, in the case of humans we read that God blessed them and *spoke to them* (Gen. 1:22, 28). Humans are thus made to be God's partners, and this partnership defines their position on earth, which extends beyond that of animals. The second creation narrative has a similar emphasis. The fact that humans name the animals shows that human beings have a say in regard to them. They are responsible before God. To that extent humans are marked out as over and above other creatures, and in a certain sense are at the centre of the community of God's creatures.

Yet this special role of human beings among the animals does not mean that God no longer enjoys a direct relationship with animals. As we shall see in more detail later, even when we are told that God says of animals, "into your hand they are delivered" (Gen. 9:2), the Old Testament does not see them as withdrawn from divine care. The Psalmist, extolling God's faithfulness and steadfast love, says, "You save humans and animals alike, O Lord" (Ps. 36:6). Even more pointedly, the Lord, speaking out of the whirlwind, asks Job:

Can you hunt the prey for the lion,
or satisfy the appetite of the young lions,
when they crouch in their dens,
or lie in wait in their covert?
Who provides for the raven its prey,
when its young ones cry to God,
and wander about for lack of food? (Job 38:39-41).

We find the same emphasis in the words of Jesus: "Look at the birds of the air; they neither sow nor reap nor gather into barns, and yet your heavenly Father feeds them" (Matt. 6:26).

All creatures, humans and animals, praise God. All creation is a single hymn of praise in which humans, animals and nature as a whole praise God with one voice (Ps. 148:7-10).

It is this creation which is termed "good" in God's eyes (Gen. 1:25), and even "very good" once it has reached completion with the creation of humankind (v. 31).

2. Violence in Creation

But is this creation really so good? Do these descriptions in Genesis 1 and 2 not apply only to an ideal state which does not exist in reality? In fact, relations between humans and animals, and even between animals and animals, are often anything but harmonious. They are characterized by force. There is a group of "tame" or "domestic" animals roundabout humans which allow people to use and exploit them. But no matter how capable they are of being the partners of human beings, they remain at the disposal of humankind. As far as these animals are concerned, human beings are their lords and masters, with power over their life and death. When people want to, they kill them. Similarly, as hunters, human beings look on undomesticated animals as their obvious prey. On the other hand, "wild animals" represent a permanent danger to humans in their immediate environment, who must be on their guard and defend themselves against them.

Violence is also a feature of the relationship between one animal and another. Animals are food not only for humans but for fellow-animals. Even when the world appears at its most peaceful, it is the stage for a permanent struggle between life and death, in which the weak succumb to the power of the strong. There is a masterly description of this process in Dino Buzzati's short story "A Peaceful Night". A couple has gone to stay in the country. One evening the husband is reading after his wife has gone to bed. Suddenly she wakes up in a fright and calls out: "I think there's someone in the garden! Have a look." To placate her he goes to the window and looks out: "What a splendid moon! I've never seen anything so peaceful!" Just then, however, a beast of prey was breaking cover. A spider was demolishing a grasshopper, and not long after that the spider was consumed by a toad which later ended up in the talons of an old owl. But the husband looking out into the garden sees nothing. "It was all lyrically, divinely peaceful." His wife wakes up again: "Carlo, I dreamed that someone was being killed in the garden." Trying to calm her, he goes to the window again: "Go to sleep, dear. There isn't a living soul outside. I have never seen such a peaceful scene."

How does the Bible see this world of violence? Not only does it take it into account, but it treats it expressly as a subject for reflection.

First of all, it is taken for granted that it is inevitable that humans kill animals and use them for food and clothing. Killing animals is part of everyday life, and there is no attempt to hide the fact that God himself made "garments of skins" (Gen. 3:21) for people. Yet we can also detect a certain aversion to the violent treatment of animals. The creation narratives maintain that killing animals was not part of God's original ordinance. They distinguish between two stages. Originally human beings were intended to be vegetarians: "See, I have given you every plant yielding seed that is upon the face of all the earth, and every tree with seed in its fruit; you shall have them for food" (Gen. 1:29). Permission to eat meat came later, and is represented as a concession on God's part: "Every moving thing that lives shall be food for you; and just as I gave you the green plants, I give you everything" (Gen. 9:3). Absolute respect for God's creatures proves impossible. In their manifestation as historical beings, humans turn out to be carnivorous.

Nevertheless, the Bible keeps the original order of things in mind. To be sure, human beings are free and able to kill animals. But from the outset God sets limits to this freedom and capability. Humankind must never forget that animals are bearers of life made by God. "Only, you shall not eat flesh with its life, that is, its blood" (Gen. 9:4). And even though humans may kill animals, their victims remain under God's protection. The covenant God made after the flood is applied expressly not only to Noah and his descendants, but to "every living creature that is with you, the birds, the domestic animals, and every animal of the earth with you, as many as came out of the ark" (Gen. 9:9-10). Now as before, humans and animals are seen as a community. A series of injunctions in the Old Testament reflect this same spirit of

concern for animals, most notably perhaps the commandment that rest on the sabbath day also applies to "livestock"
(Ex. 20:10f.; Deut. 5:14).

Second, the mystery of wild animals which threaten
humans and cattle was a constant concern of the authors of
the Bible. They represent a sphere which is somewhat
withdrawn from human control. Wild animals break into the
living space of humans and remind them how insecure and
vulnerable their life is. But the wild animals are not instru-
ments of some dark power, for they too are in God's service.
They remind people of the extent to which they are dependent on God. Wild animals can be messengers of divine
judgment. A city that falls under God's judgment is abandoned to "wild animals":

> And Babylon, the glory of kingdoms,
>> the splendour and pride of the Chaldeans,
> will be like Sodom and Gomorrah
>> when God overthrew them.
> It will never be inhabited
>> or lived in for all generations...
> wild animals will lie down there,
>> and its houses will be full of howling creatures;
> there ostriches will live,
>> and there goat-demons will dance.
> Hyenas will cry in its towers,
>> and jackals in the pleasant palaces (Isa. 13:19-22).

On the other hand, God sets bounds to the activity of wild
animals. The prophets foretell that in God's own time God
will institute peace between humans and wild animals: "I will
make for you a covenant on that day with the wild animals..., and I will make you lie down in safety" (Hosea
2:18). "I will make with them a covenant of peace and banish
wild animals from the land, so that they may live in the wild
and sleep in the woods securely" (Ezek. 34:25). And this
promise extends to the well-known vision of reconciliation
between the world of humans and cattle on one hand and that
of the wild animals on the other: "The wolf shall live with the

lamb, the leopard shall lie down with the kid, the calf and the lion and the fatling together, and a little child shall lead them" (Isa. 11:6).

Yet the Bible not only mentions tame and wild animals, but also acknowledges that the animal world extends far beyond the human environment. Though the Bible bears emphatic witness to the central position of humans in the world of animals, it is also aware that certain areas of God's creation are outside human control. This aspect of things is most heavily stressed in the book of Job: "Who has let the wild ass go free? Who has loosed the bonds of the swift ass, to which I have given the steppe for its home, the salt land for its dwelling place? It scorns the tumult of the city; it does not hear the shouts of the driver" (Job 39:5-7). Humans know only a part of creation. While everything — including animals of all kinds — is "under their feet" (Ps. 8:6), they are not actually able to exercise this "dominion". At every step, the variety of the forms of life made by God reminds them of their limitations. "Where were you when I laid the foundations of the earth? Tell me, if you have understanding" (Job 38:4).

Finally, violence among animals is seldom a theme in the Bible. That every animal will feed appropriately is assumed to be even more self-evident than in the case of human beings. God's care for the young lions and ravens is shown in their discovery of their prey. The fact that other, weaker animals must surrender their lives for this purpose hardly concerns the biblical authors. It is clearly part of God's creation that life can exist only at the cost of other life. Nevertheless, the creation story contains the astonishing statement that the animals too were originally created as plant-eaters. "And to every beast of the earth, and to every bird of the air, and to everything that creeps on the earth, everything that has the breath of life, I have given every green plant for food" (Gen. 1:30). At this point at least, violence between animals is seen as something repugnant. Though Isaiah's vision of peace in creation, which we have cited above, refers to the relationship between humans, cattle and wild animals, the indication that a time will come when the "lion shall eat straw" (Isa. 11:7) clearly reveals an expectation that God will bring all bloodshed in creation to an end. God is aware of the suffering of animals among their own kind. Their death is not simply pointless and forgotten.

3. The Fall and its Consequences

But how did the second state of creation follow on the first? What opened up the way to violence and suffering? The book of Genesis merely draws a contrast between the first and second states, but the reason for the entry of violence must be inferred from the context rather than based on any explicit statements. The assumption is that discord has its origins in humankind. By rebelling against God, humans become a source of violence — between people and between humankind and animals. Just as Cain's act of shedding blood begins a spiral of violence (Gen. 4), so humans become a threat to animals: "The fear and dread of you shall rest on every animal of the earth, and on every bird of the air, on everything that creeps on the ground, and on all the fish of the sea; into your hand they are delivered" (Gen. 9:3). And just as God sets limits to violence among human beings by putting a mark on Cain and thus preventing him from succumbing to violence (Gen. 4:15), so he restricts human dominion over animals by including them in his covenant (Gen. 9:10). The ordinance laid down by God in the act of creation is replaced by an ordinance of limited violence.

When humans transgress the boundaries laid down for them, they bring disaster on themselves and on all creation. They are capable of this because they have the gift of freedom. But animals must bear the burden of suffering. They are delivered into the hands of human beings. They become victims of humans or flee from them. Now as before they move along the pathways laid down for them by the Creator. In this respect, humans and animals are strangely contrasted. "Even the stork in the heavens knows its times; and the turtledove, swallow and crane observe the time of their coming; but my people do not know the ordinance of the Lord" (Jer. 8:7). Creation has to suffer human beings in all their violence. Regardless of how appropriate it might have seemed to bring destructive human existence to an end, God allowed people to go on living on earth. As Paul says, God himself subjects creation to the futility brought about by humankind: that is, to the disorder inappropriate to creation (Rom. 8:20). Creation lives in fear and groaning.

In his *Spiritual Exercises*, Ignatius of Loyola invites us to meditate on the astonishing fact that the heavens, the sun, the moon and the stars, the elements, fruits, birds, fish and animals support us and that the earth does not open to swallow us up (first week, second exercise, fifth part). Contrary to what should be, creation is sentenced to suffer patiently. Unlike humans who decide not to serve God, animals continue to serve humans: "The ox knows its owner, and the donkey its master's crib; but Israel does not know, my people do not understand" (Isa. 1:3).

This state of affairs can be overcome only by a renewal of humankind. Since the discord in creation originates in humanity, the way to redemption must also lead through humankind. The destruction that comes about because of the human rejection of God's ordinance can cease only if the relationship between God and humankind is restored. God's redemptive action in human beings therefore has direct consequences for all creation. The gospel proclaims good news for all creatures. They will be freed from human domination. Creation is allowed to hope that it "will be set free from its bondage to decay and will obtain the freedom of the glory of the children of God" (Rom. 8:21). This state has not yet been reached. Creation is still "groaning in labour pains" (v. 22), but a new creation free from the rule of force has already been announced.

But is this really the way we should understand all the violence that occurs in God's creation? Do the consequences of original sin actually extend so far beyond the human environment? Should we not recognize that much of what we interpret as violence has always been part of God's creation? All creation is transient. Every created thing has its own time and must die. Passing away inevitably brings suffering with it. Therefore death and suffering are not essentially meaningless. Is the same not also true of the dependence of all life on the death of other life? Surely this fact too forms part of God's good creation. Even though the Bible is opposed to violence and sees created life as under God's protection, it does not denounce this reality. No created form of life can live without feeding on other life. This applies not only to carnivores but also to vegetarians, for even though no animal needs to lose its life in order to feed them, they must kill plant life. Every creature is nourished in its own way. The idea that the lion or the spider changed its nature only because of the fall is scarcely tenable: the position of humans in creation as a whole is hardly as central as that.

God's creation is so designed that one part depends on another. Life is born from life. Life must come to an end so that new life can begin. The creation is characterized by constant dying away and coming into being. It lives by the continual sacrifice of living things. All living things — humans, animals and plants — share in this process, each in its own way. They all pass away and serve one another by their passing away. All form part of the vast sacrifice that life as a whole makes possible. In the end, no part of the whole can escape this common feature of creation.

By rejecting God, however, humans bring a new dimension into this factual state of affairs. They upset the fragile equilibrium of all creation in order to establish and implement their rule. Having exceeded the boundaries laid down for them, they then make humankind the centre of their universe to such a degree that they lose sight of the community of creation as God intended it to be. They believe that the only purpose of living creatures, animals and plants is humanity as the centrepoint of creation. The use of violence is taken as self-evident. The basic rule of creation is perverted. Instead of producing new life, humans work death and destruction.

Fundamentally, every slaughtered animal is a victim, and those who take the lives of animals must be aware that they are victimizing them. In a passage on killing animals, Karl Barth refers explicitly to this:

> The slaying of animals... undoubtedly means making use of... an innocent victim... Man must have good reasons for seriously making such a claim. His real and supposed needs certainly do not justify it. He must be authorized to do so by his acknowledgment of the faithfulness and goodness of God, who in spite

of and in his guilt keeps him from falling... He must not murder an animal. He can only kill it, knowing that it does not belong to him but to God, and that in killing it he surrenders it to God in order to receive it back from him as something he needs and desires... The killing of animals, when performed with the permission of God and by his command, is a priestly act of eschatological character (*Church Dogmatics*, III/4, §55.1).

4. "He Was with the Animals"

There is relatively little about animals in the New Testament. They are referred to incidentally in descriptions of everyday life and appear in parables and figures of speech, but they are never the express topic of any passage. Nevertheless, we may assume that the Old Testament point of view on animals was taken as valid in Judaism at the time of Jesus, and in the New Testament it is considered as self-evident. Animals belong to the human environment and are under God's special care. "They neither sow nor reap nor gather into barns, and yet your heavenly Father feeds them" (Matt. 6:26). As a whole, however, the pronouncements of the New Testament centre on the relationship between God and humanity. The fact that animals are not in the immediate field of concern is exemplified in Paul's interpretation of an Old Testament commandment in favour of animals: "You shall not muzzle an ox while it is treading out the grain" (1 Cor. 9:9). Paul cites this regulation from Deuteronomy 25:4 to support the right of the apostles to "reap material benefits", justifying his interpretation thus: "Is it for oxen that God is concerned? Or does he not speak entirely for our sake?"

More about animals and mercy towards them is to be found in the apocrypha of the New Testament. We read at one point:

> You beat animals, therefore, woe unto you not once but three times for not heeding their complaints to the Creator in heaven and their cries for mercy! Woe to those who are the cause of their complaints and cries of pain! Cease striking your beasts, that you yourself may be found worthy of mercy.

The Gospel of Pseudo-Matthew says that lions and leopards accompanied Jesus, Mary and Joseph on the flight to Egypt. There are also occasional reports of animals that renounced all force when they encountered apostles and evangelists. Thus the fourth-century Acts of Philip tell of a great leopard whose "beastlike and wild nature" was changed "into tameness".

One passage in the canonical New Testament expressly mentions Jesus' relationship to animals. At the beginning of the gospel of Mark we read an unusual and mysterious statement: "He was in the wilderness forty days, tempted by Satan; and he was with the wild beasts; and the angels waited on him" (Mark 1:13). Probably the evangelist wrote this as a way of portraying Jesus as belonging to the company of the righteous whom even wild animals cannot harm. As we read in Job: "At destruction and famine you shall laugh, and shall not fear the wild animals of the earth. For you shall be in league with the stones of the field, and the wild animals shall be at peace with you" (Job 5:22f.). Or Jesus is seen as a second Daniel, the prophet who was succoured by an angel when in danger: "My God sent his angel and shut the lions' mouths so that they would not hurt me, because I was found blameless before him; and also before you, O king, I have done no wrong" (Dan. 6:22).

In Jesus peace with wild animals as foretold by the prophets becomes reality. His resistance to Satan is the dawn of the kingdom of God. Jesus comes for the sake of humans. He is *the* human being created as God intended, and therefore his relationship with animals accords with God's original design. What the creation narrative has to say about the relationship between humans and animals becomes reality in Jesus' presence. The "community of the sixth day" is restored. It is certainly no accident that in the post-biblical period the ox and ass were introduced into the account of Jesus' birth (for the first time in the Gospel of Pseudo-Matthew) — for these are the animals capable of recognizing what human beings ignore. Recall again Isaiah's words: "The ox knows its owner, and the donkey its master's crib; but... my people do not understand" (Isa. 1:3).

To what extent, however, are we warranted in maintaining that God's redemptive action extends to the animals? The question has been posed again and again — eloquently by Swiss writer Joseph Victor Widmann (1842-1911) in his impressive poem "The Holy One and the Animals" (1905). When Jesus is faced with violence among animals, what people otherwise do not realize enters his mind: the infinite suffering of animals. The question occurs to him:

Does it have to be so? Is there no ransom that will set them free? If, on behalf of all of them, one person... but that is the very dream that often enraptures me at night, though by light of day I find it sheer empty foolishness. For no one has the only money acceptable as a ransom: the treasure of eternal life which is proof against death. A God who would die for them could pay, but no human being, no son of man, for we are all prisoners of death...

The Tempter approaches and tries to convince him that in fact this is his particular mission: "Why are you shilly-shallying? Why don't you get on with it? There they are in the sand at your feet, pleading..." Although Jesus recognizes the deception in this suggestion, that does not solve the problem. So he asks the angels, "Tell me, does my Father's vast habitation, arrayed with shining mansions, not contain a single peaceful retreat where the least of all animals can take refuge after earthly suffering?" The angels have no answer to this: "The last things are hidden from us too." He has to acknowledge that he will never understand the mystery of suffering: "I am merely wandering in an outer circle full of soulless shapes, which revolves around a hidden mystery." He has to take his leave of the suffering animals:

I too could not find the power to solve so immense a problem. So live and die as best you can. Now I must follow other paths. At least I was permitted to learn from you. You good, unassuming creatures have taught me one thing: how to be true to oneself and to bleed even though innocent.

But is this all there is to say on the subject? The Pauline references point in a quite different direction. When Paul speaks in Romans 8 of the creation waiting "with eager longing for the revealing of the children of God", he takes for granted that the redemption of the children of God is very closely associated with the redemption of creation as a whole. It is the redeemed human community who are the key to the redemption of creation. Why else would Paul picture creation as waiting for redemption? Only when human beings really become free can all creation be liberated and breathe freely. A new world will come into being. All life will not only be accepted anew but transformed by God. Humankind will not be redeemed by itself, as it were, for it will enter into glory together with the whole creation.

Thus, even in the earliest years of Christianity, Christ was associated with the Creator of the whole world. "He is the image of the invisible God, the firstborn of all creation; for in him all things in heaven and on earth were created" (Col. 1:15f.). The fact that he became a human being does not mean that God's redemptive action is directed to humans alone and that the rest of creation is excluded from it. By becoming a human being, God embraces the world. He enters into the circumstances of created life. He subjects himself to transience. He shares in the life of creation, which is characterized by domination and violence and depends for its continuing vitality on the constant slaughter of victims. By entering into the world created by God and perverted by human beings, Christ himself becomes *the* victim. It is this fact which makes all things new. "For in him," the letter to the Colossians continues, "all the fullness of God was pleased to dwell, and through him God was pleased to reconcile to himself all things, whether on earth or in heaven, by making peace through the blood of his cross" (Col. 1:19-20).

The Bible is silent about what this peace might mean in detail. Will there be a new world? Or will this present world be transformed? Will life no longer depend on the passing away of other life? Or will the creation be liberated only from destruction by domination and violence? The questions remain open. What will be surpasses all of our ability to conceptualize. But in any event, it is not human beings alone but all of creation that will be taken up into the hands of God.

5. The Meaning of Sacrifices

We turn now to a specific aspect of the subject which plays an important part in the Bible: the sacrifice of animals. Throughout the entire Old Testament it is taken as self-evident that sacrifices are to be offered to God. The notion that sacrifices of animals or of fruits of the field are acceptable to God and could seem pleasing to him is so remote from modern minds and sensibilities that we can scarcely project ourselves into the same conceptual world. Animal sacrifices now seem "primitive", something belonging to a stage of human development that we have grown out of. The idea of a temple in which animals are slaughtered and whose altar is smeared with blood now seems repulsive; and we usually tend to ignore the many passages in the Old Testament which mention sacrifices. Perhaps this is too hasty a reaction; and the use of sacrifices may be more meaningful than we generally suppose it to be. Above all, in connection with our subject in this book, we should ask what the offering of sacrifices might tell us about the relationship between humans and animals.

First of all, it is important to realize that animal sacrifices are not to be seen as acts of enmity towards animals. The practice is much more an expression of the profound union between humans and animals. Animals play an irreplaceable part in human beings' relationship with God. Only a relatively small group of animals was sacrificed in Israel. These were exclusively animals that were directly involved in the human environment: bulls, cows, sheep, doves and the like. By making a sacrifice, humans were acknowledging that everything which has life belongs to God — even those animals which seem to "belong" to humankind.

To be sure, God gave animals into human hands. They can serve people as food (Gen. 9:3). But what actually constitutes an animal's life belongs to God alone and human beings may never encroach on it. That is the sense of the commandment that the blood of any animal, whether slaughtered or sacrificed, may not be eaten. The blood of humans and of animals alike is "sacred". Humans and animals are as it were related by blood. Just as human blood when shed cries out to heaven for vengeance, the blood of animals is reserved to God (Gen. 9:4-6). Because of this relationship, animals can take the place of humans. The sacrifice of the firstborn son is replaced by the sacrifice of an animal (Exod. 34:19f.; Num. 18:15). He lives by virtue of this sacrifice. Even for Jesus, two turtledoves were offered as a sacrifice in the temple (Luke 2:24). Animals' blood has a saving and preservative effect for human beings. It protects them from evil. It grants access to God. Association with blood was of prime importance in all sacrifices offered in Israel.

What are sacrifices? So wide is the range of phenomena covered by the term "sacrifice" that any attempt at a definition is soon thwarted. Sacrifices differ so profoundly in content, intention and method that it is hardly possible to cite any common features, let alone common roots. This applies to religions in general and to the Old Testament in particular. There is no single equivalent of the word "sacrifice" in Hebrew; rather, the Old Testament presents a range of actions, each of which has its own name, to which the term "sacrifice" was later applied. It is an abstract collective term; and to give it a precise meaning we would have to examine the specific features of each sacrifice as it occurs: the Passover sacrifice commemorating the exodus from Egypt and Yahweh's saving action, burnt-offerings, communal sacrifice, the various types of expiatory sacrifice and numerous other forms of sacrifice offered for special reasons.

Each of these sacrifices has its own particular significance. In addition, the understanding and practice of it developed over a long history, not every detail of which can now be traced and elucidated. A long path led from Israel's sacrifices during the early nomadic period to those which became customary after the settlement of the promised land; from sacrifices in families and individual sanctuaries to the centralization of worship at the temple in Jerusalem; and from the experience of exile to the restoration of the temple and the minutely organized form of worship of which it became the centre. Thus the many forms of sacrifice usual at the time of Jesus represented the cumulative outgrowth of a long history.

But does Scripture itself not call into question this whole world of sacrifice and finally show it to be irrelevant? Already in the Old Testament the offering of sacrifices was subjected to radical criticism by certain prophets and in some passages in the psalms and in wisdom literature: "Of what use to me is frankincense that comes from Sheba, or sweet cane from a distant land? Your burnt offerings are not acceptable, nor are your sacrifices pleasing to me" (Jer. 6:20). Has Jesus not made the final break with offering sacrifices, and did the early church not irrevocably reject it?

On closer examination, however, it appears that the whole question of sacrifice is much more complex than this. The critique of sacrifice is not merely a matter of putting an end to sacrifice but of effecting so radical a change in its nature that any need for it as a cultic practice begins to disappear. It is also evident from the New Testament that the Old Testament tradition of sacrifice is not simply rejected but undergoes a subtle and profound transformation.

We may perhaps make this clearer by taking a more detailed look at three aspects of the issue.

First of all, the critique made by the prophets was based on the insight that the offering of sacrifices can become empty ritual, and that by relying on the outward sign of sacrifice the nation can even abandon its own responsibility before God. God looks into human hearts. People cannot hide behind the sacrifices and offerings that they make. Humans cannot rely on representation by animals. They themselves are called on to act appropriately, to "let justice roll down like waters, and righteousness like an ever-flowing stream" (Amos 5:24), to "offer to God a sacrifice of thanksgiving, and pay vows to the Most High" (Ps. 50:14). Cultic sacrifices cannot elicit grace and forgiveness, for "the sacrifice acceptable to God is a broken spirit; a broken and contrite heart, O God, you will not despise" (Ps. 51:17). The rigour of this critique is apparent in the choice of the word "acceptable"; for although the law stipulates what is needed to ensure that sacrifices are acceptable to God, they awaken only God's displeasure if the deepest intentions at the basis of the sacrifice are not fulfilled. "All deeds are right in the sight of the doer, but the Lord weighs the heart. To do righteousness and justice is more acceptable to the Lord than sacrifice" (Prov. 21:2f.; cf. Eccles. 5:1; Judith 16:16).

God is not dependent on sacrifices; he does not *need* them: "I will not accept a bull from your house, or goats from your folds. For every wild animal of the forest is mine, the cattle on a thousand hills... If I were hungry I would not tell you, for the world and all that is in it is mine" (Ps. 50:9-12; cf. Micah 6:7). Amos puts it most emphatically when he says that the sacrifices offered by the people were never mandatory: "Did you bring to me sacrifices and offerings the forty years in the wilderness, O house of Israel?" (Amos 5:25).

This line of criticism is taken further in the New Testament. The real sacrifice is human obedience to the will of God (Matt. 15:5-6). The proclamation of God's immediate presence eliminates any reason for the temple and the sacrifices made there. Why would disciples who are invited to address God with the words "Abba, Father" continue to rely on the outward signs of sacrifice? Jesus' "cleansing" of the temple by expelling money-changers and dealers is the almost inevitable consequence of this proclamation. The sacrifices consist of the disciples themselves and all that they are and have. This consideration is expressed in Paul's exhortation: "I appeal to you therefore, brothers and sisters, by the mercies of God, to present your bodies as a *living sacrifice*, holy and acceptable to God, which is your spiritual worship" (Rom. 12:1).

Second, Christ's coming especially calls into question the practice of expiatory sacrifices. The New Testament constantly reinforces the insight that reconciliation with God cannot be secured by sacrifice and offerings but only by God's liberating grace. It also continually confirms the certainty that in Christ this grace has become tangibly historical and real. Jesus lived a life of complete obedience; and in so doing he unmasked the devices of power, violence and destruction that characterize human society. By avoiding involvement in them, he himself became the target for hatred and persecution. The way he took had to end on the cross. For his disciples, however, God's acceptance of this way has become visible in the resurrection. Clearly Jesus was the servant of God who "was wounded for our transgressions, crushed for our iniquities", who "did not open his mouth, like a lamb that is led to the slaughter", the one who, "when you make his life an offering for sin, he shall see his offspring, and shall prolong his days; through him the will of the Lord shall prosper" (Isa. 53:5, 7, 10).

In him we see that God takes on himself the burden of all the consequences of disobedience: power, violence and destruction. Christ himself is the sacrificial animal: the Lamb who takes away the sins of the world. "For our sake God made him to be sin who knew no sin, so that in him we might become the righteousness of God" (2 Cor. 5:21). What meaning could animal sacrifices have now? This point is quite evident in the letter to the Hebrews: "we have been sanctified through the offering of the body of Jesus Christ once for all" (10:10). Now that he has offered himself up for us, it is clear that traditional sacrifices were no more than a semblance of the revelation to come.

The third line extends from Passover. Jesus celebrates Passover with his disciples. But while taking part in the feast which commemorated the liberation from Egypt, he also transformed the meal by using it to announce his death to the disciples: the body broken for them and the blood shed for them. The lamb that was slaughtered for the meal is now out of place. "Our paschal lamb, Christ, has been sacrificed," says Paul (1 Cor. 5:7). The eucharist recalls this sacrifice; and "as often as you eat this bread and drink the cup, you proclaim the Lord's death until he comes" (1 Cor. 11:26). The community that celebrates the meal is made free by this death; for its part, it is summoned to break through the machinery of power, violence and destruction.

Jesus Christ, the Lamb of God, is himself the sacrificial animal that was brought to the slaughter. In the book of

Revelation, the idea is developed further: the Lamb that is slain rules the whole world: "To the one seated on the throne and to the Lamb be blessing and honour and glory and might forever and ever!" (5:13). The sacrifice has brought about a reconciliation. It has restored God's ordinance in the world and opened up the way to God's kingdom. The Lamb that was slain is the true key to history. By his blood he "ransomed for God saints from every tribe and language and people and nation" and "made them to be a kingdom and priests serving our God" (Rev. 5:9-10). The expectation that was associated with sacrificial animals in the Old Testament has been fulfilled in Christ. But the sacrificial animal is still with us. The Lamb that was slaughtered serves as a symbol of the way and means by which God leads the world to salvation.

What does all this imply for the relationship between humans and animals? In a certain sense the fact that animals are no longer offered as sacrifices means liberation. Animals are freed from a role that in reality they could no longer play. They are released from the confines of the relationship between humans and God and fully acknowledged as creatures in their own right.

One other development deserves mention in this context: the questioning of the distinction between clean and unclean beasts. Jewish tradition took for granted that certain animals should not be used for food. It should be noted that the creation narrative does not mention a distinction of this kind. It even emphasizes that everything coming from God's hands is to be seen as good. But the clean-unclean distinction is certainly derived from old traditions which were included in Jewish legislation. This threat occurs in Isaiah: "Those... eating the flesh of pigs, vermin and rodents shall come to an end together" (Isa. 66:17). Jesus however puts a radical question to the distinction between clean and unclean, declaring that "there is nothing outside a person that by going in can defile, but the things that come out are what defile" (Mark 7:15). In Acts we have the plain statement: "What God has made clean, you must not call profane" (Acts 10:15).

Animals are liberated from taboos and recognized as creatures in their own specific right. The old form of community between humans and animals is unsettled and shattered. But although humans stand alone before God, their responsibility towards animals is not reduced. They have to respect the new freedom of animals. The self-evident community between God, humans and animals on which sacrifice was based has been broken up. Now it must be rebuilt on the foundations of conscious responsibility.

But will that happen? No longer bound by the old communal rules, human beings may slide into an even more uncaring domination over animals. Instead of liberation, the end of sacrifice can mean all the more suffering for animals. All depends on how firmly the image of the Lamb of God has been impressed on human hearts. Humans have to remember that life can only emerge from sacrifice and that essentially every sacrifice made by animals belongs to God himself. Human beings must arrange their lives so that they can walk before God as part of the creation for which they are jointly responsible.

6. The Witness of Saints

"And he was with the animals." For centuries the idea that the peace of Christ radiates into the animal world has remained firmly rooted in Christian tradition. Peace with animals, especially with the wild animals, was a sign of God's presence in this world.

Both in the East and the West, the legends of the saints bear eloquent witness to this. Certain saints are associated with specific animals. St Jerome is never represented without the lion at his feet watching over his prayers and scholarship. The Celtic traditions of the British Isles but also the Georgian tradition are replete with examples of saints who had a special relationship with animals, many of them hermits living alone in the forests and attracting animals from their surroundings. The 6th-century Irish saint Kieran of Saighir collected a virtual monastery of animals around him: he lived with a wild boar, a fox, a badger, a wolf and a deer. Tradition says of St Guthlac of Croyland (673-714) that "the grace of the great love of which he was possessed overflowed onto everything, so that birds of the lonely wilderness and the scattered fish of the marshes and in the water hastened to fly and swim towards their shepherd at his call; for they were wont to eat whatever food they needed from his hands". In the 12th century St Godric is said to have lived in seclusion in a forest near Durham where all wild animals were his friends. He feared neither their appearance nor their touch, and welcomed the company even of wolves and snakes and any other beast.

Saints are understood as being able to reduce the amount of violence in nature. They liberate weak animals from the grasp of their stronger foes. Wild and carnivorous creatures become tame in their presence. Every Swiss citizen knows the legend of the bear that brought wood to St Gallus. Thereafter the saint prevented it from "harming either humans or cattle". So effectively did St Francis convert the wolf of Gubbio from its ways of violence that it never again harmed any living creature.

Animals appear not only as companions but also as protectors of saints. Ravens play a special role in this respect. It was a raven that ensured that the body of St Vincent of Saragossa, variously said to have been thrown into a marshy field or cast into the sea by his murderers, was found and received proper burial. Legend also says that two ravens were loyal companions of St Meinrad of Einsiedeln, pursuing his assassins with hoarse croakings until the ruffians were arrested and executed.

A theological basis for this friendship with animals, indeed with creation as a whole, was offered by St Kentigern or St Mungo (c. 518-603), the first bishop of Glasgow:

> Before human beings rebelled against their Creator not only the animals but the elements obeyed them. But now, after the fall, because everything has taken to enmity, it is usual that the lion should rend, the wolf devour, snakes bite, the water swallow up, the fire turn to ashes, the air rot, the earth — often hard as iron — starve, and — the height of everyday evil — humans not only rise up in anger against other humans but ravage themselves through sin. But because saints for the most part are found perfect before the Lord in true innocence and pure obedience, in holiness, love, faith and justice, they so to speak recover from the Lord their old right and natural rule and hold sway over these animals, the elements, sickness and death.

Strange to say, this view of things almost entirely disappeared with the Renaissance and the beginning of the modern era. After the turn of the 16th century, scarcely anything more is heard of saints in whose spirituality community with animals plays a special part. A rare exception is Rose of Lima, the Peruvian mystic and saint (1586-1617), who joined in the songs and humming of birds and insects and performed duets with them. Since the Renaissance, it is as if animals have been banished from the company of saints. Even saints, in this respect, became people of "modernity".

The great change that occurred in the late Middle Ages was the result of a growing tendency to focus attention on humans. What is their vocation in the world? How are they intended to develop? What are their capabilities for good and evil? On the one hand, a new awareness of human mastery of the world emerged. The world became an object of human knowledge and human will. On the other hand, the evil of which humankind is obviously capable brought the question of salvation to the fore. How does God see and treat human beings who are like this and behave like this? Gradually the accent came to fall on the uniqueness of humanity. Their fellow-creatures began to fade from Christians' field of vision. So predominant did this new emphasis become that the point of view of previous centuries was no longer applicable or even comprehensible, but was dismissed as the product of a naive and no longer sustainable way of looking at the world.

7. Praise of God and Respect for Life

What does community between humans and animals mean? Undoubtedly the biblical view is far removed from the modern way of looking at things. It sounds like the description of a remote and long-lost era to which there is no return. A development has taken place which has established new conditions for the relationship between humankind and animals, and modern society has been profoundly marked by its consequences. It can function only if animals are absolutely subordinate to humans, who may do entirely what they wish with them. Quantitatively speaking, the rule of humans has gone so far that the number of victims on which they depend has risen enormously in comparison with times past.

Thus at first sight the biblical viewpoint no longer seems directly relevant to the world today. Exegetes may cite it, and historians of culture may compare it with other views in order to characterize the specific nature of Christian thought. But attempts to transpose it into contemporary terms run up against the difficulty that the problems which demand ethical decisions in the present-day situation lie beyond the bounds of the scriptural world of debate. They rely on assumptions alien to the world of the Bible. How much pain may we visit on animals? At what point may we be said to be torturing animals? What exactly is humane rearing of animals? To what extent are we bound to maintain animal and plant species? What rules are we to apply to animal experiments in scientific research? How far is it permissible to use gene technology to modify animal species? Should new species be "protected" by patents?

Questions like these arise from the fact that animals are objects of scientific knowledge and manipulation and especially of human trade and industry. But this very presupposition is called into question by the biblical point of view. The pronouncements of the Bible are so radically opposed to the perspectives of the modern age that it seems almost impossible to go back to them.

Yet the destruction brought about by technological civilization is so devastating that doubts that it is really justifiable must grow almost irresistibly. An increasing number of writers, scientists and activists are insisting that we must establish a new relationship to nature, and to animals in particular. More and more people are coming to see that endangering the survival of animals could threaten the survival of the human race as well. The fundamental question of what principles will enable us to find a way into the future is becoming ever more urgent. Perhaps the new inspiration needed in the present crisis can be discovered in the biblical understanding of God, creation. Perhaps we must risk a leap into that unknown world. It is growing increasingly obvious that a mere moderation of what has happened will not afford anything like the new direction that is necessary. A change of course in our relationship with animals is needed, something far more profound than a protest movement that amounts only to tinkering with current approaches.

To be sure, the first step is to restrict the current development by putting a stop to the most appalling excesses. Animal protection regulations and legislation and a commitment to maintain certain species are moves in this direction. But the heart of the matter has to do with the demands humans make on creation and the extent to which they are prepared to respect animals as fellow-creatures and to reduce their violence against them to a minimum. Whenever and wherever this issue is raised, the biblical view of community between humans and animals is relevant.

But what would it really imply if we were to adopt this viewpoint in our lives? The following three reflections are offered as an initial, if incomplete, response to that question.

1. The notion that animals are objects is deeply embedded in our minds and reflexes. Consequently, any attempt to escape its hold deserves encouragement. Animals can be perceived as fellow-creatures only if we actually encounter them in that way. Yet a major aspect of the degradation of animals to the level of objects is that we no longer really see them or the sacrifices they make for us with our own eyes. For many people, to be sure, domestic animals stand for the animal world; and there is no doubt that pet animals are an important initial means of access to the animal world, espe-

cially for children. Nevertheless, the image thus created is a distorted one, since pets make up only a small part of that world — a few privileged animals not only protected but maintained as companions by humans. Their very readiness to serve and submit further intensifies the idea of animals as dependent. But most people are quite unacquainted with the actual sacrifice of the countless animals that are slaughtered to feed human beings — 86 kilogrammes of meat for every person in Switzerland in 1994. Animals have become products and foodstuff. How can there be any true compassion for animals as long as we do not really see how they die? If the process of animal slaughter remains in the realm of anonymity and ignorance, the animals that serve as our sustenance will continue to be seen as products for sale rather than primarily creatures giving up their life.

2. Animal rights can be secured only if human beings exercise restraint and reduce the demands they make on the rest of creation. For many centuries the generally accepted life-style, consciously based on Christian tradition, was one of satisfaction with sufficiency. To be sure, ascetic life was not exclusively based on this consideration. Yet abstinence also meant limiting the area of creation to which human beings laid claim. In one of his homilies on the six days of creation, Basil the Great speaks of the relations between God's creatures and the fact that the strong feed off the weak. He advises human beings not to take advantage of their position of strength, but to live in the "poverty of true self-sufficiency". Asceticism is the way to a more profound relation to creation. St Francis of Assisi, often lauded as the saint of animals, was primarily an ascetic of poverty. In his case at least, self-sufficiency and openness to the animal world were closely related.

Complete or partial abstinence from eating meat is also a sign expressing something of the biblical view of the relationship between humankind and animals. This notion was scarcely unusual in the church in earlier times. St Jerome wrote in his tract against Jovinian, for example, that "until the flood... eating meat was unknown. Thereafter Moses allowed us to do so because of the hardness of our hearts. But since Christ came at the end of the ages and restored omega to alpha, taking the end back to the beginning, we no longer eat meat." Among recent theologians, Karl Barth has addressed the issue of vegetarianism:

> Yet it is not only understandable but necessary that the affirmation of this whole possibility [killing animals] should always have been accompanied by a radical protest against it. It may well be objected against a vegetarianism which presses in this direction that it represents a wanton anticipation of what is described by Isa. 11 and Rom. 8 as existence in the new aeon for which we hope. It may also be true that it aggravates by reason of its inevitable inconsistencies, its sentimentality and its fanaticism. But for all its weaknesses we must be careful not to put ourselves in the wrong in face of it by our own thoughtlessness and hardness of heart (*Church Dogmatics*, III/4, §55.1).

At a time when human demands on animals are becoming ever more problematical, the importance of this sign may indeed be all the greater.

From the earliest times, it was the practice in the Christian church to abstain from eating meat on certain days and at certain times. What was the purpose of this abstinence? And why particularly at times when Christ's passion and death were commemorated? The first consideration was certainly to foster concentration on essential things. But abstaining from meat was also a sign of peace with creation, an expression of thanksgiving for the sacrifice that Christ had made. It is no accident that it is precisely since the beginning of the modern age that these times of fasting and abstinence have been called in question and have increasingly lost their significance.

3. The Bible says that the whole creation is there to praise God. Everything from the elements of nature through plants, animals, reptiles and birds to human beings is called to join in praising the name of God (Ps. 148:7-10). This raises the question of what part this praise really plays in our life and in the life of the church. The praise described in this psalm is indeed the praise of a community of creatures that

rely on one another in order to live. They praise the Lord's name in awareness of their transience and in recognition that as they pass away they make room for new life. Human beings, too, cannot praise God without recalling the sacrifice involved in creation. Every grace before or after a meal refers to our dependence not only on the Creator but on his creation. The elements of holy communion make this clear. This joint praise of God is the deepest source of "respect for life".

Part Two:
Respect for Animals

Charles Birch

8. So Like Us

For a millennium or more most Christian views of animals were derived from non-scientific sources, in particular from the philosophical views of Aristotle and St Thomas Aquinas. According to Aristotle, only humans possess rationality: they are *anima rationalis*. But both humans and non-human animals have the capacity for feeling, *anima sensitiva*. These ideas were picked up in the scholastic tradition by Aquinas. Earlier, the Stoic view that humans have no responsibility to animals was introduced into Christian thought by St Augustine. Aristotle and Aquinas considered that animals possess no mind or reason, indeed no mental life at all. Non-rational creatures, said Aquinas, could have no fellowship with humans and therefore humans owed them no rights and bore no responsibility to them.

These views deeply coloured the attitude of Christians down the ages, putting animals low on the list of human concerns. Indeed, in the middle of the 19th century, Pope Pius IX even forbade the opening of an animal protection office in Rome on the ground that while humans had duties to fellow humans they had none to animals. As we have seen, however, in contrast to the official theology of the church many legends in popular mediaeval tradition associated saintliness with kindness to animals. Jerome had his friendly lion, as did the slave Androcles. Most famous in this respect was St Francis of Assisi, who regarded all creatures as friends to be loved and cared for in their own right. He spoke of the birds as his sisters and is said to have fed wolves. During the Enlightenment Voltaire and Rousseau espoused a compassionate attitude to animals. On the other hand, Immanuel Kant declared in his lectures in 1780 that animals are not self-conscious and exist only as means to human ends. In the same year Jeremy Bentham gave what has been described as the definitive answer to Kant: "The question is not can they reason? nor can they talk? but can they suffer?" Bentham anticipated the day when the whole of the animal creation would acquire those rights which could only have been withheld from them "by the hand of tyranny", and when the mantle of humanity would extend over everything that breathes. Arthur Broome, who was responsible for founding the first animal welfare organization in the world in 1824, the Society for the Prevention of Cruelty to Animals, spoke about the extension of Christian compassion to animals. The society early affirmed its foundations on Christian principles. Yet the history of human attitudes to animals is largely discouraging, considering that it took nearly 2000 years for humans in the West to agree that it is wrong to be cruel to animals.

Our modern understanding of animals, based on studies of animal behaviour, stands in strong contrast to the views of Aristotle, Augustine and Aquinas which dominated thinking about animals for so long. This is brought out strikingly by the title of a recent authoritative book on the behaviour of animals: *Animal Minds*, by Donald Griffin of Harvard University. So we ask in the light of this new knowledge, do animal have minds? Do they reason? Are they conscious? Are they *self*-conscious? Do they suffer pain?

Are animals conscious?

Just as most of the functioning of the human brain occurs without our conscious awareness, this is also the case with non-human animals. But it is highly probable that non-human animals do experience conscious thoughts about their activities. This applies particularly to the ways in which they communicate.

One of the clearest examples of communication in animals which suggests conscious thinking is the alarm calls of the vervet monkey. These monkeys live in groups in forests and open areas in Africa. When they see dangerous predators they make three different alarm calls in response to three sorts of predator: leopards, eagles and snakes. The alarm call for a leopard causes vervets to run into trees where they seem safe from attack; the alarm call for an eagle causes them to look up into the air or to run into bushes; the alarm call for a snake causes them to stand on their hind legs and look into the grass. By recording each of these three sorts of alarm calls and playing them back to vervets in the wild, it is possible to elicit the corresponding response in the absence of any predator. This indicates that it is the call and not the sight of the predator to which they are responding. One call means climb a tree. Another means look in the air. Another means look in the grass. The three different calls are symbols that have three different meanings to vervet monkeys. Linguists use the word "semantics" to mean the attribution of meaning to symbols. These three sorts of alarm calls thus function as semantic signals for the monkeys, suggesting conscious thinking on their part.

Experiments on the way apes can be trained to communicate with each other and with humans by means of symbols indicate a similarity between human and ape communication and thinking, despite the fact that only humans have verbal language. Apes have been taught to use more than 100 signs developed for deaf people. But they cannot express these symbols as spoken words.

Many mammals, especially those we have as our companions, seem to experience pleasure, pain, terror, fear, suspicion, jealousy, self-complacency and pride, as we do. They sulk. They love their children. They are curious and adventurous. They become lonely. They grieve. Jane Goodall, who spent many years studying chimpanzees on the Gombe Reserve in Africa, came to the conclusion that chimpanzees are intelligent animals with a rich and varied social and emotional life:

> The postures and gestures with which chimpanzees communicate — such as kissing, embracing, holding hands, patting one another on the back, swaggering, punching, hair-pulling, tickling — are not only uncannily like many of our own, but are used in similar contexts and clearly have similar meanings. Two friends may greet with an embrace, and a fearful individual may be calmed by a touch, whether they be chimpanzees or human. Chimpanzees are capable of sophisticated cooperation and complex social manipulation. Like us, they have a dark side to their nature: they can be brutal, they are aggressively territorial, sometimes they engage in a primitive type of warfare. But they also show a variety of helping and care-giving behaviours and are capable of true altruism.

Goodall reports a number of occasions on which chimpanzees she observed seemed to grieve. When Flint's mother died, this young chimpanzee exhibited many patterns of behaviour we associate with grief in humans. He avoided others, stopped eating and spent many hours each day sitting in a hunched posture rocking back and forth. Not long afterwards he died.

The songs of birds give pleasure to humans. But do they give aesthetic pleasure to birds? Prof. Charles Hartshorne, who recorded bird songs around the world, became convinced that these songs are structured in a way that avoids monotony. A bird that is capable of producing only few notes spaces them further apart than one that has many notes. Indeed the musical construction of bird songs is parallel to what is found in our own music. Facts like these have convinced Hartshorne that birds *enjoy* bird song.

There are at least six reasons why students of animal behaviour attribute consciousness to non-human animals. We shall do no more than list them here to indicate that there is a body of evidence from different sources which, taken together, leads to the conclusion that non-humans, like us, are conscious:

1. Their behaviour is similar to behaviours of ours which we know to be conscious for us.
2. Their physiology and biochemistry are similar to ours.
3. Adaptable behaviour is explained more simply and directly by assuming that it is conscious.
4. Complex means of communication between animals suggest that they are conscious.
5. Humans have evolved from creatures who were non-humans, for the most part by a gradual step-by-step process. Evolutionary innovations do not come into existence full-blown. They have a history.
6. Animals have a point of view in which what happens to them matters to them. Animals care about what happens to them. This suggests that they are conscious about caring.

Anxiety and suffering

The more we know about non-human animals, the more similar to ours their physiology and biochemistry seem to be. For example, anti-anxiety agents (benzodiazepines) have an effect on non-human animals similar to that which they have on us. Sensory receptors for these chemicals have been found in all vertebrates except sharks. This suggests that a wide range of vertebrates experience some sort of suffering akin to anxiety in humans. Nervous systems and sense organs exist in all animals from jellyfish to humans, but even single-celled animals such as amoebae are sentient. All life is sentient. It would probably be true to say that gradations in sentience are related to the complexity of the nervous and sensory system of the particular organism.

How much does a non-human animal suffer? While there is no simple way of measuring suffering, we do have some clues. Some suffering in animals is caused by stress. A sheep confronted by a dog or confined in a small pen exhibits the first indication of stress, which is the alarm phase. It secretes stress hormones from the adrenal glands, which give rise to flight or fight. The heart rate increases as does the rate of breathing. For an animal in the wild, such as a zebra being stalked by a lion, this is the stage when the animal runs away or attacks. If the stress continues, as it would for an animal confined in a small pen, another set of hormones is secreted from the pituitary gland in the head, leading to the second phase of stress, known as the resistance phase. The body is now provided with an additional source of energy such as sugar. Eventually the animal enters the final stage of stress, which is exhaustion. The animal slows down, resistance to disease is lowered, digestion is impaired and stomach ulcers may develop.

These symptoms typically occur when animals are crowded in cages or are transported in cruel ways. We can infer that these animals are suffering. One wonders what sheep experience when thousands of them are transported in pens on ships from Australia to the Middle East. In mid-1996 a ship containing 70,000 sheep on one of these long voyages caught fire in the Indian Ocean. The crew escaped in lifeboats, but the blazing ship drifted on until it sank, with all the sheep on board either burned to death or drowned.

On the basis of similarities in physiology between humans and non-human animals, the American Veterinary Medical Association has recognized the following sorts of suffering in animals:

• *Pain:* an unpleasant experience of the senses and emotions associated with damage to parts of the body.

• *Distress:* a state in which an animal is unable to adapt to an altered environment (such as abnormal food) or an altered internal state (such as high blood pressure).

• *Discomfort:* a state in which an animal seems unadapted to a new environment — such as being transported or being removed from its kin.

• *Anxiety:* a state of increased arousal and alertness prompted by an unknown danger, such as a cat might experience on a visit to the veterinarian.

• *Fear:* a response to the presence of a known danger such as a predator in the immediate environment.

An animal may experience a number of these states at the same time. For example, an animal in pain often exhibits distress and may also become fearful if in strange surroundings such as a vet's surgery. The above analysis can help veterinarians and others who have dealings with animals to recognize the different ways in which animals suffer and thus also how such suffering can be avoided.

Intelligence

But can animals reason? Evidence for intelligent behaviour is the ability, quite common among birds and mammals, to adapt complex behaviour to varying and often unpredictable circumstances. A hungry chimpanzee walking through the rain forest comes upon a large nut of the panda tree lying on the ground. These nuts are too hard to open with the hands or the teeth. They can be cracked by pounding them with a hard rock, but very few rocks are available in the forest. However, the chimpanzee walks straight to another tree some 80 metres away where he had managed several days earlier to open a panda nut with a chunk of granite. He carries the rock back to the nut he has found, places the nut in a crotch between two roots and cracks it open with a few well-aimed blows. This is intelligent behaviour.

A green-backed heron breaks a twig into small pieces and uses it as bait for fishing. It casts the twig into the water and watches it intently until an unfortunate minnow investigates, and the heron dives on it. The behaviour of the heron is quite flexible. She may drop the bait from an overhanging perch or from the water's edge, retrieving it if it floats away. This too is intelligent behaviour.

But what about the minds of simpler animals such as insects? We now know that honeybees use complex dances on the honeycomb to communicate with each other both the distance and direction of food from the hive and the concentration of the source they have discovered. The bees do not appear to be acting as programmed robots, for this behaviour is not totally stereotyped. If honeybees communicated this information with words rather than dances, and if they were the size of dogs, we should no doubt be strongly inclined to attribute to them similar experiences as we have when someone else tells us to go to this place or that. On the basis of his extensive studies of the behaviour of honeybees over a lifetime, Donald Griffin is convinced that there are good reasons to attribute consciousness to them and that animals of many different kinds think, remember, anticipate, intend, suffer and enjoy life.

Self-consciousness

Students of animal behaviour make a distinction between the awareness of something like the presence of food and reflection on that awareness. The latter is called self-consciousness. It means not only knowing but knowing that one knows. Self-consciousness is thinking about one's feelings and thoughts. While a human infant is aware of many things such as hunger, pain and touch, reflection on these perceptions comes only later in life. But even though all mature human beings reflect to some extent on what they are aware of, the degree of reflection various immensely. A hermit in his cave presumably does an enormous amount of reflection compared to a drinker in the corner tavern. This difference in degree of reflection suggests that there may also be gradations in self-awareness as we go from humans to the various apes and perhaps even further down the scale. There is no reason as yet to draw a sharp line anywhere.

If an animal reflects it would be difficult for us to know, because it has no language to tell us. However, some chimpanzees can recognize themselves in a mirror, as contrasted with cats, which cannot — suggesting that chimpanzees are self-conscious. In one experiment, some chimpanzees who had become familiar with mirrors were made unconscious and a mark was placed on a part of the head which they could not see directly. On awakening they paid no attention to the mark until a mirror was provided. Then they touched the mark and gave every indication of recognizing that the mark was on their own bodies. They must have reflected that it had something to do with themselves. Orangutans also respond to mirrors in this way, but efforts to elicit such responses from monkeys and gibbons and gorillas have not been successful.

The point of this excursion into animal behaviour is to illustrate that animals have minds that can be conscious and even self-conscious in some cases. They show rationality or intelligent behaviour. They experience joys and sufferings. They are more like us than we have understood until now. In short, they are not mere objects, but subjects. As such, they deserve our respect; and from this it follows that we have a responsibility for their well-being.

The philosopher Thomas Nagel has written a widely read essay called "What is it like to be a bat?", in which he concludes that there is such a gulf between him and a bat that he cannot know what it would be like to be a bat. Nagel is saying that the subjective experience of a bat is the bat's alone and not his. But would he come to a similar conclusion about his cat or dog? Of course, I cannot know what it is really like to be my cat in the sense that I know what it is like to be me. Nor can I know directly what it is like to be you. I cannot have your experience. What I can do is to empathize with you: to infer, when you say and do certain things, that my experience of similar things leads me to understand to some extent your feelings. We can do the same with those animals which we have as companions whom we know better than bats. Avid cat-lovers know a lot about the feelings of their companions. This sort of understanding strikes a chord of empathy among cat-lovers.

There are those who will retort that all this is a form of anthropomorphism, which means looking at all creatures through human eyes. But we ask, what is wrong with that and what else can we do? Indeed, a crucial way of interpreting the world around us is to take human experience as a high-level example of the nature of reality in general all down the line. Instead of calling this anthropomorphic it is better to call it a life-centred approach, which recognizes the centrality of human experience in understanding the world. Anthropomorphism should not be confused with anthropocentrism, which sees the human being as "the measure of all things".

Are humans unique?

While we have a great deal in common with non-human animals, humans are nevertheless unique in several characteristics. Our uniqueness is mostly a matter of degree. The philosopher Alfred North Whitehead said "the distinction between us and non-human animals is in one sense only a difference in degree. But the extent of the degree makes all the difference. The Rubicon has been crossed." It is unlikely that, if one could place in a long row all our human ancestors, from some ape-like creature through the ape-men to ourselves, one would be able to draw a sharp line anywhere and say "here is the first human". Verbal language, which is unique to humans among all living creatures on earth today, may have begun before *Homo sapiens*, perhaps in *Homo erectus*. But humans today have complex languages by means of which they communicate with one another. The development of language made a complex culture possible, for culture is the knowledge which one generation passes on to the next. Human feelings lead to a richness of experience that may be presumed greater than that of other species. Moreover, humans reflect on their experience in their self-consciousness to a degree that seems exceptional. Humans are also pre-eminently rational creatures. They have a degree of freedom to choose which is probably greater than in other creatures. Their capacity to choose values gives them a moral sense.

The scholastics maintained that only humans had souls, by which they meant that aspect of us which survives the death of the mortal body. But there is no reason to deny that the lives of non-human creatures contribute to the life of God and have an eternal value to God. In that way they too would participate in immortality. When Jesus said that not a sparrow falls to the ground without God's knowing, he seemed to be suggesting that the sparrow has a value to God. And if it has a value to God, then it contributes to the life of God. We shall return to this topic in the next chapter.

We tend to view living things quite differently from dead things or material objects such as rocks and chairs. What makes the difference is that we feel at least a germ of empathy with living things. We imagine ourselves feelingly in their place. We wonder at their possible pleasures, pains, desires and interests. Besides being interesting to us or others, the living creature presents itself as interesting to itself. So Robert Frost writes about "A Considerable Speck":

> A speck that would have been beneath my sight
> On any but a paper sheet so white
> Set off across what I had written here.
> And I had idly posed my pen in air
> To stop it with a period of ink,
> When something strange about it made me think.
> This was no dust speck by my breathing blown,
> But unmistakably a living mite

With inclinations it could call its own.
It paused as with suspicion of my pen,
And then came racing wildly on again
To where my manuscript was not yet dry;
Then paused again and either drank or smelt —
With loathing, for again it turned to fly.
Plainly with an intelligence I dealt.
It seemed too tiny to have room for feet,
Yet must have had a set of them complete
To express how much it didn't want to die.
It ran with terror and with cunning crept.
It faltered: I could see it hesitate;
Then in the middle of the open sheet
Cower down in desperation to accept
Whatever I accorded it of fate.

I have none of the tenderer-than-thou
Collectivistic regimenting love
With which the modern world is being swept.
But this poor microscopic item now!
Since it was nothing I knew evil of
I let it lie there till I hope it slept.

I have a mind myself and recognize
Mind when I meet with it in any guise.
No one can know how glad I am to find
On any sheet the least display of mind.

What are the implications of finding that animals lead emotional lives comparable to ours and that many of them show intelligent behaviour? In their book *When Elephants Weep*, Jeffrey Masson and Susan McCarthy respond to this question with the following further questions:

> Must we change our relationship with them? Have we obligations to them? Is animal testing defensible? Is experimentation on animals ethical? Can we confine them for our edification? Can we kill them to cover, sustain and adorn ourselves? Should

we cease eating animals who have complex social lives, passionate relations with one another and desperately love their children?

These are some of the questions that we explore in chapters 9 and 10.

9. How Much
   Is an Elephant Worth?

'Twould ring the bells of Heaven
The wildest peal for years,
If Parson lost his senses
And people came to theirs,
And he and they together
Knelt down with angry prayers
For tamed and shabby tigers
And dancing dogs and bears,
And wretched, blind pit ponies,
And little hunted hares.

The tamed and shabby tigers, the dancing dogs and bears and the little hunted hares of Ralph Hodgson's poem are still with us. And if the blind pit ponies are gone, there are now hens in battery cages and animals on "factory farms". Non-human animals are an oppressed group in the modern world.

The movement for animal rights has arisen out of concern for the suffering that human beings inflict on individual animals, chiefly domestic ones. This concern has direct parallels with the movement for human rights. The most fundamental of human rights is the right of every human person to live. Killing people is wrong. The argument for such a moral affirmation is that every human being has a value in himself or herself and to God irrespective of any usefulness he or she may have to others. This affirmation that humans are not simply means to useful ends, but are ends in themselves, is known as the intrinsic value of every human being. Theologically, it has been undergirded by the concept of *imago Dei* — that humans are created in the image of God.

Intrinsic value

Christians have tended to regard respect for life as an exclusive human right and have drawn a line here between humans and all other animals. But is this right such an exclusive human possession? We have almost entirely regarded animals as having instrumental value for us. They are valuable to us for their food and fur, as workhorses and as companions. But are these their only values? The considered answer now must be that non-human animals have their own intrinsic value just as humans do. They have value in themselves, to themselves and to God. They have an inborn urge to live, which expresses the value their own lives have to them. Furthermore, the message of the creation account in Genesis is quite clear: before there were any humans there were non-human animals, and God declared them to be good. They had value to God quite independent of any value they would later have for human beings.

Christians emphasize the appeal to the *imago Dei* of Genesis as exclusive to humans. It is true that the biblical account does single out human beings as those for whom God is peculiarly concerned. But the accent Christians have put on this reflects an unwarranted arrogance whose source is not a balanced reading of the biblical story. The context of the creation story in Genesis focuses on the goodness of the whole creation. God pronounced that the whole lot was "very good". That can surely imply nothing other than that non-human creatures have their own intrinsic value to themselves and to God.

We can be more precise about what gives intrinsic value to every human individual and every living creature. Tables and automobiles and computers are useful objects. They are means to our ends. That is to say they have *instrumental value* to us. But they are objects only and not subjects and therefore have no intrinsic value in themselves. Only subjects have *intrinsic value*. What gives them intrinsic value is that they feel. Only feelings confer intrinsic value. It is not only humans who feel the world. So do all sentient animals. Their feelings may be very different from ours, but they do have feelings.

The difference between animals and humans lies in what we could call richness of experience. The richness of a cow's experience as it grazes in the pasture may be fine for it. But if that were the sum total of our experience we would feel very deprived. Jay McDaniel identifies two components of richness of experience in our own lives. One is harmony, which is a feeling of accord and affinity with ourselves, with other people, with other creatures and with God. A second component is zest, which might also be called energy, vitality, enthusiasm or compassion.

Among human beings there are differences in richness of experience from one person to another and from one moment to the next. Human experience includes all experiences of value and the experience of God. Some would go so far as to say that any experience of value is an experience of God, for God is the source of all values. Without being a cow or a mosquito, I can hardly make statements about what constitutes the richness of their experience, though it could surely be argued that the avoidance of suffering and the promotion of harmony would be desirable experiences for them. With a bit of imagination we can apply the same criteria to other animals as well. Konrad Lorenz, the student of animal behaviour, said no one could assess the mental qualities of a dog without having once possessed the love of one. And he added that for himself this also applied to jackdaws, parrots, geese and monkeys.

We noted in the previous chapter that some would dismiss this line of thinking as anthropomorphic — describing non-human animals in human categories — but that we can hardly do otherwise. Each of us knows himself or herself to be conscious of pain and joy and many other feelings. But not one of us has the feelings of anyone else. I can only imaginatively infer that others have similar feelings to mine. My own consciousness is my privileged avenue into the appreciation of the feelings of other people. The same principle applies to the less competent knowledge we have of other animals. We in the modern world need more, not less, of this "anthropomorphic" thinking about other creatures if we are to understand and appreciate their world.

God and sparrows

If we believe that all experience of value eventually derives from God, then we can say that, in their own way, non-human animals surely experience God. "Not a sparrow falls to the ground without God's knowing" is a statement about animals attributed to Jesus. This means that even the lone sparrow has some value to God; that God *feels* its life and the closing of it. If the sparrow's life is an experience *for* God, then it must also be an experience *of* God. In the teaching of Jesus a human life is said to be of more value than many sparrows (Matt. 10:31). That does not warrant the conclusion that a sparrow is worth nothing at all; rather, it implies that if a human being is worth many sparrows, then a sparrow's worth is not zero. The account in the gospel of Luke adds: "and not one of them is forgotten before God" (Luke 12:6). Here the implication is that if God cares for the sparrow, how much more must God care about human life. And God cares for all.

Does God experience the sparrow? This question implies the need for creation-inclusive theology, in which God makes a difference to each of us and to every creature, and each of us and every creature make a difference to God. In the classical version of theism promoted by Aristotle and many others after him, by contrast, God does not experience or suffer. For Aristotle God was the "unmoved Mover". God moves everything but is moved by nothing. Part of what Aristotle had in mind was the doctrine of internal and external relations. Process theologian David Bromell explains this with the example of a pillar and a cat. The cat has an *internal* relation to the pillar, because the pillar makes a difference to the cat. It provides shade from the hot sun and a hiding place from which to pounce on its next meal. But the pillar has only an *external* relation to the cat. It makes not the slightest difference to the pillar that the cat exists. Aristotle concluded that God is more like the pillar than the cat. God makes a difference to all of us and to the whole creation, but not one of us nor even the whole of creation makes a scrap of difference to God. Throughout the whole evolution of the cosmos from the Big Bang to us, God has never experienced, never suffered, never changed.

But in a creation-inclusive theology God knows when the sparrow dies and grieves and laments over the suffering and injustice in the world. As Cyril Vincent Taylor puts it in his hymn "God is love":

> God is love and *he enfolding*
>   *all the world in one embrace,*
> with unfailing grasp is holding
>   every child of every race.
> And when human hearts are breaking
>   under sorrow's iron rod,
> then they find *the selfsame aching*
>   *deep within the heart of God.*

Elie Wiesel tells the story of the hanging of two Jewish men and a young boy by SS guards at Auschwitz in front of the whole camp:

> "Where is God? Where is He?", someone behind me asked... But the third rope was still moving; being so light, the child was still alive.
>
> For more than half an hour he stayed there, struggling between life and death, dying slowly in agony under our eyes. And we had to look at him full in the face...
>
> Behind I heard the same man asking; "Where is God now?"; and I heard a voice, "Here he is — hanging there on this gallows."

God, who is present in the suffering and agony of the child on the gallows, is present in the suffering of all God's creatures, including the non-human animals of the creation.

Means and ends

We live in a community of subjects. The animals around us should therefore be treated not merely as means but as ends in themselves. The Genesis account of creation implies an ordering of intrinsic value of animals above plants, and humans above other animals. Otherwise the authors would hardly have considered it morally acceptable for animals to eat plants and humans to eat plants and animals (Gen. 9:3). At the same time, the recognition of the intrinsic value of all animals clearly implies the expansion of compassion and justice to them all.

Two stories from the Old Testament may help to illustrate this concept of the intrinsic value of animals. One is the parable told by the prophet Nathan to David after the king committed adultery with Bathsheba and had her husband Uriah killed so that he could marry her. The prophet's story is of a rich man with many sheep of his own, who nevertheless steals his poor neighbour's single lamb to provide a meal for an unexpected guest. The poor man had bought this lamb and "brought it up, and it grew up with him and with his children; it used to eat of his meagre fare, and drink from his cup, and lie in his bosom, and it was like a daughter to him" (2 Sam. 12:3). Hearing this story, the king (who has not yet figured out its application to his own case) is enraged: "He said to Nathan, 'As the Lord lives, the man who has done this deserves to die'" (v. 5). As the valued pet of the poor man, which he loved as one of his own children, the lamb had a great instrumental value. For the rich man to take its life was to deprive the poor man of a certain richness of experience in his life. But in addition to the lamb's instrumental value to the poor man, it had a value in itself to itself and to God, which we call its intrinsic value. Thus in the killing of the lamb two sorts of value were annihilated.

The second story is the extraordinary account recorded in Numbers 22 about a prophet by the name of Balaam who saddles his donkey and rides off on a dubious mission. Suddenly the animal stops short and turns off the road into the field. Balaam strikes the donkey, but it refuses to go on and scrapes Balaam's foot against a wall. When he strikes it again the donkey lies down underneath him. But then the donkey also speaks to Balaam: "What have I done to you, that you have struck me these three times?" Balaam replies: "Because you have made a fool of me! I wish I had a sword in my hand! I would kill you right now!" To this outburst the donkey retorts, "Am I not your donkey, which you have ridden all your life to this day? Have I been in the habit of treating you this way?" And Balaam ashamedly replies, "No." According to the story, the donkey stopped because it saw an angel standing on the road with a drawn sword. Not until Balaam replied to the donkey were his eyes opened so that he too could see the angel. Balaam is scolded by the angel, who tells him that if the donkey had not turned back it would have been Balaam who would have been killed, since the errand he was on was displeasing in God's eyes. A critical element of this story is that the donkey is presumed to have experiences not unlike those of its master. It says to Balaam in effect, "You have hurt me. How would you like this done to you?" That is the correct context within which to think about our attitude to animals. *How would you like this done to you?*

The conservation laws of most countries recognize the *instrumental* value of plants and animals, as they should. Four sorts of instrumental ethics are invoked by conservationists. These have been summarized as (1) the "silo" argument for maintaining the availability of all those species which are useful to us for food, medicinal and other purposes; (2) the "laboratory" argument for maintaining a supply of those organisms which some scientists say are needed for experimental studies; (3) the "gymnasium" argument of nature for leisure; and (4) the "cathedral" argument of nature for aesthetic pleasure. All of these provide empirical reasons for being concerned about plants and animals alike.

But it is high time that conservation laws also recognized the *intrinsic* value of creatures. So far only one country in the world — Aotearoa New Zealand — incorporates the phrase "intrinsic value" in its conservation legislation. This degree of ethical enlightenment was to a considerable extent a result of the influence of the so-called deep ecologists. It is also an insight that is in harmony with the biblical tradition. For when Proverbs 12:10 says that "the righteous know the needs of their animals", there are two reasons for this. One is the value of the animals to them — in any of the ways mentioned in the previous paragraph. The other is the intrinsic value of the animal — in itself, for itself and to God.

The rights of animals

Why do other people matter? Because we respect them. But on what foundation does this respect stand? We believe that we owe respect to other human beings because we respect their intrinsic value to themselves and to God, however we might express this. Another way to put this is to say that human beings are ends in themselves, not simply means to other ends. So, too, we should respect the lives of animals because they too have an intrinsic value.

These affirmations can also be expressed in the language of rights. We say that human beings have among other rights the right to live. This statement expresses the judgment that all human beings should be viewed and treated in a certain way, and not simply according to our personal tastes or preferences. It affirms that there are inherent characteristics in human beings which ground and require this judgment. So we affirm that murder of the innocent is always wrong, that rape is always wrong, that child molestation is always wrong, that sexual and racial discrimination are always wrong. Whenever I have a duty towards others, that is, whenever I ought to treat others in a certain way for their own sake, I can make the same point by saying that those others have a *right* to be treated in that way. So, too, we affirm that non-human animals have the right to live, as well as other rights, such as the right not to be subject to unnecessary suffering. This obliges each of us to accept certain duties to non-human animals. The argument that rationally grounds the rights of humans also grounds the rights of non-human animals. Both are cut from the same moral cloth.

Next we must ask how absolute these rights are. In the case of human beings we tend to regard the right to live as absolute. We also consider slavery to be wrong, even though it took the best part of 1900 years for Christian theologians, among others, seriously to question the morality of slavery. It is now universally agreed that it is the absolute right of a human being not to be a slave. In slavery human beings become property in the strict sense of the term. This is sometimes referred to as "chattel slavery", a term that stresses the parallel between the human institution of slavery and the ownership of animals, for the words "cattle" and "chattel" are derived from the same roots. In this context cattle were seen as slaves to human ends.

There is much dispute today about how to respect the human right to life in two particular situations: at the beginning of human life and near the end of human life. At the beginning the dispute revolves around abortion; at the end the dispute revolves around euthanasia, the right of terminally ill patients to seek to end their own lives. These are complex and contentious issues which it is not our purpose to explore here, although the problems they raise cannot be ignored by Christians. As far as non-human animals are concerned, abortion is not an issue. Rather, those who are concerned with plagues of rabbits and feral animals appropriately investigate the possibility of control by chemical sterilization. And at the other end of the life-span, most people have no compunction about ending the incurable suffering of a companion animal by euthanasia, "putting it to sleep".

But how absolute is the right of animals to live? We can answer this question only if we recognize that there is a gradation of rights within the animal kingdom, which reflects the gradation in intrinsic value of the animal and which, as we have suggested, depends on its capacity to feel. In chapter 8 we indicated that this capacity exists from the lowliest creature to the highest, from the amoebae to the great apes to humans. It then follows that there is a gradation of animal rights along this sequence.

We have less compunction about killing a mosquito or an oyster as compared with a bird or a mammal. Indeed, we kill mosquitoes by the millions to get rid of malaria in human societies. This seems acceptable. In technical terms we might say that the instrumental value to humans of malaria-carrying mosquitoes is negative. Each mosquito has its own tiny intrinsic value, but the sum total of that intrinsic value is outweighed by the negative instrumental value to us. Although we may never make this sort of calculation consciously, we would be aware of the reasons for our action in such a case. If four human beings and a dog are in a lifeboat and all will die unless one of them is thrown overboard, it would surely not be wrong to throw the dog overboard in these dire circumstances. Even though the one dog has its real and substantial intrinsic value to itself and to God, no one would doubt that the life of one human counts more than the life of one dog.

The rights of animals include more than the right to live. They also have the right not to suffer unnecessarily. If any animal feels pain, that pain matters, just as it does to one of us. Pain is pain whatever the individual species that experiences it. If a pig experiences a pain which is equivalent in suffering to a pain I may experience, then I should be equally concerned. The "if" in this sentence is important. We can never know exactly how severe the pain of a pig might be, but we can use our imagination. When my cat suffers from kidney cholic and appears to be in agony, I have some inkling of what it is going through, because I too have suffered from kidney cholic. And I am concerned.

In the case of the malarial mosquito, the right of humans to live free of disease dominated the equation. But this bias is not necessarily always the case. In the United Kingdom, the Wildlife and Countryside Act of 1981 accorded the bat special protection in law. Even in competition with humans, bats are given preferential treatment. It is illegal for anyone without a special licence to kill, injure or handle a bat of any species or to disturb a bat in its nesting place. Individual householders are prohibited from disturbing nesting bats on their roofs even if they are causing damage or creating a risk of disease. The use of any pesticide or wood preservative that could harm the bats is prohibited. Licences to destroy bats can be given only after investigation and consultation with a third party, which normally recommends nonviolent preventive measures.

The rights of animals and the rights of humans are often in conflict. Many were shocked by stories of Japanese fishermen who were bent on slaughtering porpoises, which they regarded as competitors for fish. The worldwide reaction in turn shocked the fishermen, who had taken their anthropocentric ethical principles for granted. While it is legitimate to side with the critics of these Japanese fishermen now, what if the time comes when the fish of the sea become scarce and Japanese people are threatened with starvation as a result? It is easy to predict that if we do not exterminate porpoises altogether by a completely anthropocentric policy, we will reduce their numbers drastically. In African countries today, the question arises whether wilderness should be preserved in sufficient quantity to secure the survival of many species of wild animals. Land set aside for this purpose cannot be used to grow crops to feed Africa's growing human population. Some years ago, for example, Rwanda had to choose between having elephants in national parks or using this area as farmland for people. In the end, it was decided to airlift at least some of the elephants to a national park in a neighbouring country. It seems that a positive intrinsic value was given to the elephants, which they tried to save in this way.

Christian perspectives on our responsibility to animals

The sixth assembly of the World Council of Churches (Vancouver 1983) called for an emphasis in Council programmes on justice, peace and the integrity of creation. One facet of the somewhat unfamiliar concept "integrity of creation" could be the recognition of the integrity of the intrinsic value of every living creature and the maintenance of the integrity of the relations of each creature to its environment. A great deal of human activity is destructive of the life and relations of non-human creatures. We have broken the bonds of nature that bind every creature.

The appropriate word for the restoration of a broken relationship is salvation. This is an ecological word, because it is about restoring a right relationship that has been corrupted. After I had addressed the fifth assembly of the WCC (Nairobi 1975) on these and related matters, the conference newspaper published a story headlined "Salvation for Elephants". That was appropriate. For in the biblical and early Christian understanding, salvation is basically a cosmic matter: the world is to be saved. Basil the Great evidently thought so when he included animals within this context in one of his prayers: "And for these also, O Lord, the humble beasts, who bear with us the heat and burden of the day, we beg you to extend your great kindness of heart, for you promised to save both humans and beasts, and great is your loving kindness." St Isaac the Syrian also extended the meaning of compassion in a similar way:

> What is a charitable heart? It is a heart burning with love for the whole creation, for humans, for birds, for beasts, for demons, for all creatures. Those who have such a heart cannot see or call to mind a creature without their eyes being filled with tears by reason of the immense compassion which seizes their heart; a heart which is softened and can no longer bear to see or learn from others of any suffering, even the smallest pain being inflicted on a creature...
>
> That is why such persons never cease to pray also for the animals, for the enemies of truth and for those who do them evil, that they may be preserved and purified. They will pray even for reptiles, moved by the infinite pity which reigns in the hearts of those who are becoming united with God.

From the Christian point of view there is also the perspective of God on the whole of life. This includes God's perspective on both human beings and on animals, extending, as we saw earlier, to the life of the sparrow. The implication is that each creature makes its distinctive contribution to the divine life. God experiences the gustatory delights of humans eating their veal; God also experiences the lifelong misery of the calves that produce the veal. The former falls far short of balancing the latter. Millions, indeed billions, of creatures will continue to suffer unnecessarily unless we understand that suffering is evil in itself and causes suffering to God as well.

The Christian is called on to be a neighbour to those in need, not to cross by on the other side but to attend to the victim on the side of the road. We can extend the meaning of this parable to non-human animals in need. We can seek to be neighbour to non-human animals in a way quite analogous to the way we seek to be neighbour to our fellow humans in need: to succour those who fall by the wayside, to try to remove the causes of suffering, to provide room in the inn. In many countries every large city has people who do just that for stray cats and dogs whose owners have abandoned them. In the outskirts of Sydney, for example, there is an animal refuge called The Fund for Animals, which takes in cats and dogs who have no home and seeks to find homes for them. But so far as I know, no animal refuges in cities are run by churches. Why not?

Animals cannot speak for themselves and defend their rights. In this respect their status is analogous to that of children and to humans who because of infirmity cannot defend their rights. Adult humans thus have a special responsibility to children, the infirm and non-human animals. All these cases put a greater claim upon us precisely because of their powerlessness and vulnerability. The English animal rights activist Andrew Linzey calls this the "generosity theory" of animal rights. According to this view we are called upon to show respect, care, love, generosity and compassion to animals. One could argue that animal liberation will require greater altruism on our part than does any other liberation movement, since animals are incapable of demanding it for themselves or of protesting against their exploitation by votes, demonstrations or bombs.

The Judaeo-Christian scriptures have been used to warrant three basic attitudes towards animals, which might be summarized in three words: exploitation, stewardship and compassion. In exploitation only instrumental value is ascribed to non-human creatures. While stewardship adds the element of responsibility, it still ascribes no more than instrumental value to non-human creatures. Only the third attitude ascribes intrinsic value to individual creatures; yet in recent centuries it has been the least dominant attitude in Western Christianity.

One reason for this is that Christians have tended to interpret Scripture anthropocentrically, denying value and rights to non-human life. Some of this can no doubt be traced back to the fact that the doctrine of *imago Dei* has been understood to mean that humans alone are created in the image of God. The proper context of this doctrine in a creation-inclusive theology has largely been lost during the course of Christian thought. A second reason for the reluctance of Christian churches to accept responsibility for the whole creation is their prior concern for the poor and oppressed. But why should a concern for oppressed and suffering animals detract from the consideration of the basic human needs of the poor and oppressed human beings? If a concern for humanity were held together with a concern for the creation at the same time, the human perspective might then come closer to the divine perspective on the creation. It should be remembered that the humanitarian reformers who have spoken out most strongly for animals — among them Voltaire, Wilberforce, Shaftesbury, Bentham, Mill and George Bernard Shaw — have been front-rank campaigners for the rights of human beings as well.

While many Christian churches and theologians have been slow to move towards a concern for all living creatures and to recognize the intrinsic value of non-human life, there are exceptions. One is the eco-justice movement in some Protestant churches in the United States, which brings together concern for justice with an environmental concern. The World Council of Churches has had programmes in the area of a just and ecologically sustainable society for more than two decades, though as yet it has not explicitly recognized the intrinsic value of non-human animals. The International Network for Religion and Animals in the United States seeks to open dialogue with religious communities about the value of non-human life and ways to reduce suffering caused by humans and to develop a religious perspective on the value of all life. The Glauberg Confession, an ecumenical statement issued by a group of Christian clergy and laity in Europe, acknowledges guilt and feelings of shame for our failure to care for the non-human animals with which we share this world. Its final sentence reads: "As the church, we were deaf to the groaning in travail of our mistreated and exploited fellow creatures." The United Church of Christ in

the USA has made "A Pronouncement on Christian Responsibility Toward Animal Creation", which deals with the
historical failure of Christianity adequately to consider
humanity's proper relationship to and responsibility for the
animal creation. In twenty pages, it develops both a theology
of concern for animals and its practical consequences. The
Christian Consultative Council for the Welfare of Animals in
London arranges conferences and consultations on the Christian responsibility to non-human animals. The International
Fund for Animal Welfare (IFAW) has established in Mans-
field College in Oxford the world's first academic fellowship
in the ethical and theological aspects of animal welfare.

Perhaps relatively few people in our time are yet willing
to become ambassadors for a new consciousness towards the
other species who share the earth with us. But that puts the
onus even more squarely on those who become committed
and on churches in particular, whose convictions should lead
them in this direction.

The great achievement of the Enlightenment was to build
a theory of human rights that made possible enormous
advances towards social justice. A great achievement of our
time could be to extend the concepts of rights and justice to
all living creatures, not only in theory but in the practice of a
non-anthropocentric, life-centred ethic based on a creation-
inclusive theology.

10. What To Do?

US Patent No 47366866, dated 12 April 1988 and entitled "Transgenic Non-Human Animals", protects the property rights of the creators of "oncomouse", a mouse produced by genetic engineering which contains a sequence of genes that makes it highly susceptible to cancer. The purpose of creating oncomouse was to facilitate research into causes of cancer in humans.

At least ten countries now permit animal patents, while another 50 or so have not prohibited the granting of such patents. There are at least two ethical concerns here. One has to do with the recognition that patenting a living organism seems to put it into the category of objects, like new mechanical inventions, whereas animals are subjects with their own feelings of the world. Biotechnology companies, which spend heavily on research into new developments in genetic engineering, claim that if they are not protected by patent rights they will be unable to recoup their investments and compete in international markets. Once again we see here the familiar conflict between economic advantage and moral considerations.

A second issue has to do with suffering of manipulated animals. Oncomouse will no doubt be the subject of the usual kinds of experimentation with mice and as such is likely to suffer some degree of pain. We do not know how it feels about being an oncomouse. We might perhaps have a better idea of how another genetically engineered mouse might feel — one which grew to three-and-one-half times the normal size of a mouse. And we know even more about sheep that have been engineered to grow to huge sizes with the aid of a genetically induced growth hormone. The purpose of the exercise was to have sheep with a large surface area so that each sheep could grow more wool. But early experiments with such sheep had to be abandoned because of their disturbed physiology, which caused them much suffering.

Some would object to any suffering we may cause sheep. Others try to balance possible gain to humans against what the sheep have to suffer. One can imagine that in the future some poultry farmers might wish, for marketing reasons, to

produce chickens with four drumsticks instead of a mere
two. All of these examples, real and hypothetical, raise the
question of what sort of alteration of an animal is ethical.

Experimentation on animals

For a century or more, animal breeders have used artifi-
cial selection to breed cows that produce more milk, bulls
that produce more meat and chickens that lay an egg a day.
On the whole this programme of animal breeding has gone
on without much public attention. Is there a fundamental
difference between this selective breeding and change
through genetic engineering? Experiments in genetic
engineering raise large ethical problems, some of which we
have already mentioned. Churches should become aware of
these problems and try to help to provide guidelines for these
technologies which would take into account the feelings and
intrinsic value of animals involved.

Genetic engineering is only one special case of
experimentation with animals. For many other purposes
more than 100,000 vertebrates are used in research
laboratories all over the world. Eighty-five percent of these
are rats and mice. Frogs, pigeons, hamsters, rabbits, dogs,
cats, pigs and primates make up almost all the rest. About
five percent are used for teaching purposes, another five
percent for diagnosis of disease, twenty percent for production of biological substances such as growth hormones and
for toxicity testing, thirty percent in the development and
testing of drugs and forty percent for other research activities
such as genetic engineering.

A quite recent form of animal experimentation is the
investigation of animal-to-human transplants of organs such
as hearts and livers. The basic question here, says Andrew
Linzey, is "whether we are right to look upon other sentient
creatures simply as walking spare parts for human beings".
Once benefit to humans is established by a new technology
involving non-human animals, we too readily assume that
what is good is identical to what is good *for us*. But there are
other considerations.

A Dutch survey indicates that fifty percent of all animal experimentation involves a risk of appreciable discomfort to the animals. Those who totally reject animal experimentation argue that any suffering to animals is unacceptable. Those who favour total acceptance argue that the suffering of animals in experimentation is the price to be paid — by the animals — for human benefit. Others take up an ethical stance somewhere between these two extreme views. Much more has been published on total rejection than on all the other views. While the ethical issues here are complex, a minimum requirement is surely that animal experimentation should not be undertaken without counting the cost in suffering to the animals involved. Another minimum consideration — as in the case of chimpanzees (now classified as an endangered species) — is whether the cost to be paid may be the possible extinction of the species.

A special case of the use of animals in laboratories is for testing a huge variety of household products and health and beauty aids that humans use — toothpastes, cosmetics, colognes and after-shaves lotions, deodorants, detergents, window cleaners and the like. These products are routinely tested on animals in a variety of painful ways including eye-irritance tests and so-called lethal-dose tests, in which the toxicity of a product such as a deodorant is established by force-feeding it to animals until 50 percent die. Both these sorts of tests have been prohibited in some parts of the world, including the Australian state of Victoria. After the cruelty of some of this sort of testing was revealed in the media, there was an outcry worldwide from those concerned with the rights of animals. As a result, there are now more and more products on the market which have been tested without using animals, and this number would increase further if consumers demanded them rather than products involving tests on animals.

The ultimate objective regarding all animal experimentation is to do away with it altogether. There are alternatives. One is the use of tissue culture, which is the growth of animal (including human) tissues in glass containers such as

Petrie dishes. The manipulations are then done on cultured tissue rather than on live animals. Other alternatives are also being developed.

Because of a greater appreciation of the ethical issues involved in animal experimentation, most countries in the Western world have ethical review committees which determine acceptable standards for housing of laboratory animals and experimentation on them. As a consequence, we know that many experiments, especially some which were done on monkeys in the past, would now be considered completely unacceptable. It is only through the efforts of those working to protect animals that progress of this sort has been made. Much more remains to be done. Churches should align themselves with watchdog organizations that monitor the treatment of animals in laboratories in their own community to make sure that these activities are responsible and fair to both the animals and would-be experimenters. One would hope that a consequence of this greater sensitivity would be that at some point in the future all experimentation on animals is replaced by alternative procedures.

Meat production

Even more than experimentation on animals, however, the human practice of meat-eating is probably the major cause of animal suffering in the world today.

In the United States alone, more than four billion animals are raised for slaughter each year; and much of this relies on what are called "closed confinement" or "intensive rearing" methods. For the most part these animals are raised indoors, with no sunlight and sometimes without even room for them to turn around. Virtually all of the 239 million laying hens in the US are confined for their entire lives to small cages in which they cannot turn around or stretch their wings. Many breeding sows are kept for as long as five years in stalls barely larger than their body. Veal calves are routinely taken from their mothers at birth and raised in permanent isolation. Increasingly, even dairy cattle are being taken off the land and raised indoors.

Additional suffering is caused when these animals are transported to slaughterhouses or to the market. The cruellest process is live export. Australian sheep, for example, may be transported overland to docks as far as 2000 kilometres away from where they were raised. The road trip may take up to four-and-a-half days, during which the sheep are packed so tightly that they cannot move or lie down. More stress follows when they are loaded onto ships for their final destination in the Middle East or Southeast Asia. During the long ocean voyage, on ships which may hold as many as 125,000 sheep, the animals are exposed to severe changes in the weather and for most of the time they cannot lie down. In 1994, about 100,000 sheep — two percent of the total exported — died during transit in Australia, en route to their overseas destination or upon arrival. We noted in chapter 8 that some 70,000 sheep died in a single ship fire on the high seas in 1996.

Despite public protest, this trade has gone on since 1945; and it is of considerable economic importance: each year Australia ships some 5.5 million live sheep and 700,000 live cattle to Indonesia, the Philippines and Malaysia. Similar live exports occur in other parts of the world. Only action by national governments will stop it, and that in turn depends on concerted and ceaseless public protest.

To purchase the products of corporate factory farming is to support massive animal deprivation. But there are alternatives. We can choose to buy products from the remaining small-scale family farms and buy eggs from free-range hens, which are increasingly available in supermarkets and other shops. We can explore a dietary life-style that is free from all direct commercial connections with the suffering of animals. We can support legislation against cruel methods of raising animals. Perhaps the most telling response is to become vegetarians.

Largely in response to the activities of animal liberation groups, Sweden and Switzerland have passed legislation to phase out the battery-cage system of keeping hens. Sweden has also planned to rid itself of the worst forms of factory-farming for pigs and cattle. The standard methods of raising calves for veal has been declared illegal in Great Britain and in at least one Australian state.

Above and beyond the argument of the suffering caused to animals, there are good reasons to question the promotion of increasing meat consumption in the rich world. Sound health practices would suggest a higher vegetable component in the human diet in the rich world. Meat production is also a wasteful way of producing food. More than 90 percent of the oats, corn, rye, barley and sorghum grown in the US is fed to animals — an enormous waste, since only one-tenth of the plant products that animals eat is converted into meat.

But there is further environmental waste involved in eating large quantities of meat. Since 1960 more than 25 percent of the forests of Central America have been cut down to allow cattle to graze where the trees once stood. For many years, it was said that every hamburger eaten in the United States meant the destruction of about eight square metres of forest. While US imports of beef from Central America have declined in recent years, the cattle industry there continues to engage in deforestation. And in Brazil, cattle ranchers are still pushing on, oblivious to the plants and animals which are destroyed as they burn and bulldoze the Amazon jungle. After a few years of cattle grazing, the soil loses its fertility, the pasture is abandoned and scrub takes over. The forest does not return.

As the human population of the world continues to increase, people will have to eat less meat and more vegetables in their diet. We should anticipate this change, which has long been part of life in developing countries.

All the animals in the Genesis creation story are vegetarian. The animals live on grass and the humans live on nuts and fruit. It is only when the humans become evil that they turn into enemies of other animals and regard them as food. The famous passage in Isaiah cited earlier looks forward to a day when paradise is regained, everyone goes back to a non-meat diet and the friendliest relations subsist between species:

The wolf shall live with the lamb,
> the leopard shall lie down with the kid,
the calf and the lion and the fatling together,
> and a little child shall lead them.
The cow and the bear shall graze,
> their young shall lie down together;
and the lion shall eat straw like the ox...
They will not hurt or destroy
on all my holy mountain;
for the earth will be full of the knowledge of the Lord
> as the waters cover the sea (Isa. 11:6-9).

This passage has been interpreted in different ways, but in any case it does suggest that predation and meat-eating raised theological problems for these early writers. They recognized that individual animals matter, and they looked forward to an age when not only would humans live in peace with the other animals — not eating them or contesting with them — but also the other animals would no longer prey on one another. All would be vegetarians.

This desire for human beings and the beasts to live in peace is reflected in the ancient story of Androcles and the lion. According to the legend, a battle with wild beasts on a grand scale was put on for the Roman people at the Great Circus. One of the beasts was a huge lion. A slave named Androcles was brought into the arena. When the lion saw him from a distance, he stopped short as if in amazement, then slowly approached the slave, wagging his tail. Gently he licked Androcles' feet and hands. It seemed that the two recognized each other.

The emperor, wishing to know why the lion had spared the slave, summoned Androcles, who told him how he had run away from his master into the desert where he had taken refuge in a remote cave. A lion came into the cave with a bleeding paw, groaning and moaning in pain. Androcles said the lion had approached him mildly and gently lifted up his foot, as if asking for help. The slave had taken out a huge splinter and cared for the foot. The lion had then put his paw into Androcles' hand, lain down and gone to sleep.

Subsequently both Androcles and the lion had been captured and brought to Rome, where the slave was condemned to die in the arena. Upon hearing the story, the emperor, after a vote of the people, freed both lion and man. They walked the streets together and everyone marvelled at the lion that was a man's friend and the man who had been a physician to a lion.

Furs and entertainment

Another group of animals that are subjected to cruelty are those which are killed for their fur. Some 100 million animals are trapped worldwide for this purpose; many others are raised on fur-farms, where they live in unnatural conditions similar to those of factory farms, in which their ability to move and form normal social units is severely limited if not entirely restricted. In the US some 17 million animals are trapped annually — beavers, lynx, fox, mink, raccoons and muskrats. Trapped in the wild, they suffer slow and agonizing deaths.

Alternatives to fur are becoming more evident as pressure is put on furriers to change their trade to non-animal clothing. The campaigns of animal liberationists have made the wearing of fur virtually unacceptable socially in Britain and the Netherlands. Here the choice of the Christian would seem to be obvious: avoid buying clothes made from the coats of animals and work for laws against the sale of furs.

Another source of cruelty to animals is their use for entertainment in zoos, circuses, gladiatorial shows and hunting. The morality of confining animals for display and entertainment should be sharply questioned: the day of wire cages and concrete pits should long ago have passed, but it has not yet. A recent series of television documentaries on the private and public zoos in Europe shocked many viewers, who had no idea of the miserable conditions in which animals live in many zoos. What is claimed as the educational role of zoos has been superseded by an increasing number of superb wildlife films, made in the natural habitats of the animals. Zoos have a role in saving threatened species, but perhaps for little else.

There is also no room in a life-centred ethic for performing animals in circuses. The same goes for cock-fighting and bullfighting, which remain legal forms of entertainment in some countries. Mary Midgley has cogently remarked that bull-baiting has not been replaced by bulldozer-baiting because active personal conflict is what the crowds want to see in such "sport".

Hunting for entertainment is a primitive activity pandering to crude emotions. Recreational hunting accounts for the shooting and killing of about 200 million mammals and birds each year in the US. That number includes a wide variety of birds, black, brown and grizzly bears, coyotes, mountain lions and wolves. Open seasons for shooting wild ducks and other wild fowl cause great suffering, much of it in the form of lingering death. Every duck-shooting season in the states of Australia is accompanied by considerable protest from animal liberation groups who have alerted citizens to the cruelty involved. In the state of New South Wales this has resulted in ending open seasons for duck hunting.

Australia has a particular problem with kangaroos, which are so abundant in the eastern states that farmers regard them as serious pests and call for their destruction. This great increase in the number of kangaroos has resulted from damming and other practices by which farmers provide ready sources of water for their sheep. So kangaroo hunters come in and shoot kangaroos, then sell their meat and hides. As a result of this legal culling process, some two million kangaroos are shot each year — the largest slaughter of a single kind of native animal in any part of the world. There is no doubt that this involves tremendous suffering to the dying animals and their abandoned joeys.

A similar increase in numbers of a native species because of farming practices also occurs in other parts of the world — for example, the increase in the deer population in some states in the midwestern United States has led in some cases to legal "culling" by hunters of what are regarded as excessive populations of deer.

There are alternative possibilities which animal liberationists have tried to promote. In the case of the kangaroos in eastern Australia, one scheme has been to return the land to kangaroos and take away the sheep. This is not quite as radical as it may sound; and already huge estates of millions of hectares in the western part of New South Wales have been returned to kangaroos after the expiration of 99-year leases to farmers. This has happened only as a result of pressure placed on the government by sectors of the public to increase the extent of wildlife reserves and wilderness areas.

In response to the concern that this is unfair to farmers, it should be noted that the programme has been facilitated by the fact that these areas ought never to have been turned over to sheep farming in the first place. While there are few problems in good years, during the inevitable periods of drought the sheep eat every bit of vegetation on the land, including the bark of whatever trees remain. Left bare, the soil surface is eroded by the winds, leaving huge unvegetated sand dunes. This does not happen when only native animals occupy the region.

That in turn leads some to argue for the farming of native animals — kangaroos in Australia and antelopes and the like in parts of Africa. Here again the issues are complex. It is true that in both of these cases, the native animals do much less damage to the land than domesticated hoofed animals. On the other side of the ledger is the fact that this would mean the introduction of abattoirs and slaughtering for species that have not previously been subject to mass killings, which many people would regard as the extension of an existing horror.

Fishing is a specific form of hunting which must be regulated in many places if the species are not to be reduced to dangerously low levels. This presents a problem for indigenous peoples, who depend on fishing as a major source of food. Their traditional methods of harvesting are more likely to be conservative of the species, and they may thus present a lesser threat to the species than modern methods and attitudes. In Australia, Aboriginal peoples who depend on native animals for their livelihood are granted exemptions from laws against fishing. A case in point is the dugong, a wondrous mammal of tropical waters also known as a sea cow, since it grazes algae. Although it is highly protected in Australian waters, in some places this protection is waived for Aboriginal groups.

Commercial fishing fleets with their highly mechanized procedures have become a threat to many marine fish species. The long trawling lines and huge nets used by some fleets also present a threat to albatross and dolphins. The next commercial step, one would imagine, would be the creation of vacuum cleaners of the sea, which would simply suck up everything that came along. Technological developments in this direction warrant total opposition. Fish harvesting in the future will have to be more, not less selective if we are to protect the biosphere.

Extinction and biodiversity

The story of Noah and the flood emphasizes the preservation of not only individual animals but also of species. "Keep them alive with you" (Gen. 6:19) was the injunction given to Noah when he was told to build the great ark. Moreover, the covenant God established with Noah after the flood, whose symbol is the rainbow, included "every living creature that is with you, the birds, the domestic animals and every animal of the earth with you, as many as came out of the ark" (Gen. 9:10).

The extinction and decline in number of animal species has become horrific in the modern world. This is due mainly to the destruction of habitats, especially forests, by humans. A tragic example is the destruction of forests in Africa, mostly by European companies, which has led to the killing of many gorillas and chimpanzees. Fewer than 300,000 chimpanzees survive in the world and the number of gorillas is much smaller. The logging companies make remote forests accessible to hunters for the first time. As a result the killing of previously safe wild animals has made the sale of "bush-meat" in towns and villages a big business in Africa. In one district of Cameroon, an estimated 800 gorillas are being killed each year.

Recently a group of people sympathetic to the plight of the nearest relatives of humans among the animals — chimpanzees, gorillas and orangutans — have established the Great Ape Project, which seeks to work for the end of the destruction of their habitats, of poaching, of their use in research, of their exhibition in zoos and their use as objects of entertainment. Because of what we now know about the lives of the great apes, the project goes further and argues for the inclusion of the great apes within the sphere of equal moral consideration with humans. Great apes are intelligent beings with a rich and varied social and emotional life. They are like us even in their genetic makeup: we share 98 percent of our DNA with the two living species of chimpanzees.

The general consensus of ecologists is that by the end of this century, the earth will have lost, through human destruction of habitats, between 29 and 50 percent of its species of all forms of life. Over the past decade, the rate of species extinction has increased from one per day to one per hour. Most of these are plants. At this rate, from half a million to several million currently existing species are likely to perish by the year 2000. A quarter of the world's mammals are on the list of endangered species, which includes 33 percent of primate species, 11 percent of bird species, 25 percent of amphibian species and 20 percent of reptile species. The United States now ranks among the 20 countries with the most endangered species; Madagascar and the Philippines have the largest percentage of endangered species.

Some species are facing huge declines in their numbers. Over the past twenty years, the number of elephants in Africa has declined from 3 million to 700,000. The white rhinoceros population has dropped from 1500 to 12. There were 10,000 Asian tigers in 1940 and 4000 in 1970. With protection, their numbers have now increased to about 7500.

Whale populations are between 3 and 25 percent of what they were before whaling became industrialized. Once there were more than 250,000 blue whales, now there are 500; once there were more than a million humpback whales, now there are 10,000; once there were 100,000 white whales, now there are 4000. There is no question of the need for continued protection through a total ban on whaling.

The existing international moratorium on whaling is difficult to maintain, because the smaller minke whale has rising populations, now totalling several hundred thousand. Japan and Norway, who ignore the moratorium of the International Whaling Commission (IWC) on hunting whales, argue that stabilizing the number of minke whales by hunting could assist the recovery of the endangered whale species. Others are quite sceptical of this reasoning. For this reason, the arguments of anti-whaling nations for maintaining the moratorium have begun to shift from the need to save endangered species to other objections to killing whales, which emphasize their intelligence, their majesty, their complex communication and social life. So it was a great advance at a recent IWC meeting in Kyoto, Japan, when the US representative said it would not support the resumption of whaling even if the number of whales would permit it.

For similar reasons, some countries, among them Australia, have prohibited the capture of dolphins in their waters. We now know that dolphins are highly intelligent animals that have a rich social life as a result of their wonderful ways of communicating with each other. Their social groupings survive as such for many years, and one can only imagine what they may suffer when these social groups are broken down by deliberate or accidental destruction as a result of careless fishing. Possibly, it is not just the individual dolphin that is killed which suffers but the whole group of which it was a member.

The chief cause of species extinction, however, is the destruction of habitats by humans. The human race is extremely greedy for land. For food, fodder and timber, human beings and domestic animals consume about four percent of the total plant production on land. Yet an even greater proportion of plant production on earth is diverted into human needs, such as the widespread replacement of natural communities with human-created ones. All this multiplies the total human impact on terrestrial plant production to the amazing figure of more than 30 percent. So if we were to triple our impact through population and economic growth, we would be using close to 100 percent of the total terrestrial plant productivity of the earth for ourselves, even though we are only one of about 30 million species of animals.

The great diversity of species on earth is referred to as the earth's biodiversity. Plants, animals and micro-organisms are organized in communities such as rainforests and grasslands. The organisms in these various communities, on earth and in the sea, provide services which enable life to continue on earth. Many people do not realize that these life-support systems are responsible for the following free services:

— maintenance of the gaseous composition of the atmosphere;
— control of the provision of fresh water through the water cycle;
— detoxification and disposal of wastes;
— cycling of nutrients, such as nitrates, for replenishing the soil;
— control of pests and diseases;
— pollination of crops and wild plants;
— maintenance of a vast "genetic library", which is a resource for future agricultural crops, medicines and industrial materials.

Yet the organisms that are responsible for the maintenance of the life-support systems are threatened with a colossal extinction because of human destruction of habitats. We know the role of only a few of these organisms, so we are not in a position to say which ones are essential and which are not. In the face of our ignorance on this score, what should be our attitude?

In their book *Extinction* (1981), Paul and Anne Ehrlich address this question in the form of a parable:

> As you walk from the terminal towards your airliner, you notice a man on a ladder busily prying rivets off its wing. Somewhat concerned, you saunter over to the rivet-popper and ask him just what he is doing.
>
> "I work for the airline, Growthmania International," the man informs you, "and the airline has discovered that it can sell these rivets for two dollars apiece."
>
> "But how do you know you won't fatally weaken the wing doing that?", you enquire.
>
> "Don't worry," he assures you. "I'm certain the manufacturer made this plane much stronger than it needs to be, so no harm's done. Besides, I've taken lots of rivets from this wing and it hasn't fallen off yet. Growthmania Airlines needs the money; if it didn't pop rivets, Growthmania wouldn't be able to continue expanding. And I need the commission to pay me fifty cents a rivet!"
>
> "You must be out of your mind!"
>
> "I told you not to worry; I know what I'm doing. As a matter of fact, I'm going to fly on this flight also, so you can see there's absolutely nothing to be concerned about."

The Ehrlichs go on to say that they would cancel their flight on Growthmania Airlines and book on another carrier. But you never *have* to fly on an airliner at all. However, all of us are passengers on a very large spacecraft — one on which we have no choice but to fly. "And frighteningly," say the Ehrlichs, "it is swarming with rivet-poppers behaving in ways analogous to that just described." Rivet-popping on Spaceship Earth consists of aiding and abetting the extermination of species and populations of non-human organisms.

The natural ecological systems of earth which supply the vital services for life are analogous to the parts of an airliner that make it a suitable vehicle for human beings. But ecological systems are much more complex than rivets and wings and engines. A dozen rivets, or a dozen species, might never be missed. On the other hand, the thirteenth rivet popped from a wing — or the extinction of a key species involved in the cycling of nitrogen — could lead to an eco-catastrophe.

The United Nations Conference on Environment and Development held in Rio de Janeiro in 1992 produced a Convention on Biodiversity to give a lead to all nations of the world to take urgent steps to preserve the diversity of species. The monumental *Global Biodiversity Assessment* commissioned by the United Nations Environment Programme (UNEP) in 1995 is an 1149-page document to which some 1500 scientists contributed. It represents a consensus of the relevant scientific community on biodiversity. Its foreword says:

> Biodiversity represents the very foundation of human existence. Yet by our heedless actions we are eroding this biological capital at an alarming rate. Even today, despite the destruction we have inflicted on the environment and its natural bounty, its resilience is taken for granted. But the more we learn of the working of the natural world, the clearer it becomes that there is a limit to the disruption that the environment can endure.
>
> Besides the profound ethical and aesthetic implications, it is clear that the loss of biodiversity has serious economic and social costs. The genes, species, ecosystems and human knowledge which are being lost represent a living library of options available for adapting to local and global change. Biodiversity is part of our daily lives and livelihood and constitutes the resources upon which families, communities, nations and future generations depend.

Can the churches heed this plea no longer to take the resilience of nature for granted? There are thousands of communities throughout the world who are working to preserve biodiversity in their local areas. In Australia alone there are a thousand such communities committed to save the creation. The call to the churches is to do likewise. The emphasis is twofold: protect nature because nature protects us, and protect individual creatures because each one has intrinsic worth to itself and also to God.

According to an legend recorded in the Talmud, when God decided to create the world, he said to Justice, "Go and rule the earth which I am about to create." But it did not work. God tried several times to create a world ruled by

Justice. But each time it failed and the earth was destroyed. Finally on the eighth day, God called Mercy and said, "Go together with Justice and rule the world I am about to create, because a world ruled by Justice alone cannot exist." This time the earth survived just because there were enough people who saw to it that some justice and mercy prevailed.

Ideals and practical steps

The teaching of biology in schools and colleges often involves the dissection of animals such as frogs and rats. Students who resist this for reasons of conscience should not be coerced to do what they object to. Indeed, alternatives now exist that should be used by all students. These include detailed drawings of anatomy and physiology and even computer programmes that enable students to "dissect" a frog or another mammal on the screen. There are also excellent nature films that show animals in their natural habitats and provide knowledge that was unavailable to previous generations.

The extent of suffering and death to animals in the world today is immense. Much of it is due to our human life-style. Many of the things that can be done to reverse this have been mentioned in this chapter. We need also to extend our values of life to include all the living creation. Instead of an anthropocentric ethic we need to shift to a biocentric or life-centred ethic. That involves a concern for the quality of life of those animals who share our earth with us. We need to modify our life-style, especially our consumer habits.

We should involve ourselves in changing social and political policies to enhance the lives of animals. We desperately need a reordering of our economic systems so that they take account of animals as ends in themselves and not just as means for human ends. So far, very little consideration has been given to this aspect of economics, which has primarily focussed on economic growth — be it of livestock, automobiles or any other commodity. Much economic growth today is at the expense of the environment, of future generations of human beings and of animals. We should insist that the economy be ordered not to its own expansion but to the well-being of humans and animals. That means the end of factory farming and cattle feedlots and hens in battery cages. It will mean a new sort of economics.

Such an economics would take into account the following principles articulated by the Humane Society, one of the leading organizations promoting animal welfare in the US:

— It is wrong to kill animals needlessly or for entertainment, or to cause animals pain or torment.

— It is wrong to fail to provide adequate food, shelter and care for animals for which humans have accepted responsibility.

— It is wrong to use animals for medical, educational or commercial experimentation or research unless absolute necessity can be demonstrated and unless this is done without causing the animals pain or torment.

— It is wrong to maintain animals that are to be used for food in a manner that causes them discomfort or denies them an opportunity to develop and to live in conditions that are reasonably natural for them.

— It is wrong for those who eat animals to kill them in any manner that does not result in instantaneous unconsciousness. Methods employed should cause no more than minimum apprehension.

— It is wrong to confine animals for display, impoundment or as pets in conditions that are not comfortable and appropriate.

— It is wrong to permit domestic animals to propagate to an extent that leads to overpopulation and misery.

The serious application of these principles, which are modest enough, would enormously reduce the suffering we now inflict on our fellow creatures. To be sure, they would involve significant changes in many of our practices, particularly in farming. Yet they represent a bare minimum of requirements. Many advocates of animal rights would call for the abandoning of all experimentation on animals, the adoption of a vegetarian diet and the banning of all use of animals in entertainment. Christians have a responsibility to decide where they stand on all these issues of mercy and justice.

Christians are called on to act with respect and reverence towards these "the least of our brothers and sisters". This is not just an act of mercy but of justice as well. As we have mentioned earlier, Paul speaks in Romans 8 of the whole of creation as groaning in labour pains until now. The passage then goes on to say that the liberation of nature is directly linked to the emergence of God's new family, who are already experiencing the fruits of the Spirit. The passage links the redemption of nature with the redemption of human beings. It does not say, "Save people and they will save the world." Rather, it is saying that redeemed people have an obligation to save the world. These ancient texts speak eloquently to our own time and circumstances. The animals have been groaning, and we have not heard them. Let us hear them now as they cry out to us for mercy and justice.

The fall of humanity is not just an event in the long-distant past. It occurs at every moment when our actual life falls short of the creative possibilities for that moment. It occurs when we fail to respect and show reverence to the non-human creation. It has always been this way.

For those who think that the task of the liberation of the environment and the animals in it is too daunting, it is helpful to recall the words of Margaret Mead, who was instrumental in helping to establish the work of the World Council of Churches in the area of environmental issues: "Never doubt what a small group of thoughtful committed citizens can do to change the world. Indeed, it is the only thing that ever has."

Some Suggestions for Further Reading

Charles Birch, William Eakin and Jay B. McDaniel, eds, *Liberating Life: Contemporary Approaches to Ecological Theology*, Maryknoll NY, Orbis, 1990.

John B. Cobb, *Matters of Life and Death*, Louisville, Westminster-John Knox Press, 1991.

Donald R. Griffin, *Animal Minds*, Chicago, Univ. of Chicago Press, 1992.

Andrew Linzey, *Animal Theology*, London, SCM Press, 1990.

Among the sources for accounts of the saints and animals are the following: *Acta Sanctorum*, Paris and Rome, 1863-1868; Joseph Bernhart, *Heilige und Tiere*, Munich, 1937; Sister Mary Donatus, *Beasts and Birds in the Lives of Early Irish Saints*, Philadelphia, 1994; Lieselotte Junge, *Die Tierlegenden des Heiligen Franz von Assisi (Königsberger Historische Forschungen*, vol. 4), Leipzig, 1932; C. Plummer, *Vitae Sanctorum Hiberniae*, Oxford, 1910; Helen Waddel, *Beasts and Saints*, London, 1934.

Risk
BOOK SERIES

The Risk Book Series from WCC Publications deals with issues of crucial importance to Christians around the world today. Each volume contains well-informed and provocative perspectives on current concerns in the ecumenical movement, written in an easy-to-read style for a general church audience.

Although any Risk book may be ordered separately, those who subscribe to the series are assured of receiving all four volumes published during the year by airmail immediately upon publication — at a substantial savings on the price for individual copies. In addition to the four new titles each year, occasional "Risk Specials" are published. Although subscribers are not automatically sent these books as part of their subscription, they are notified of their appearance and invited to purchase them under the same advantageous conditions.

If you wish to subscribe to the Risk series, please send your name and address to WCC Publications, P.O. Box 2100, 1211 Geneva 2, Switzerland. Details and an order form will be sent to you by return mail.

Some of the titles to appear recently in the Risk Book Series are:

James B. Martin-Schramm, *Population Perils and the Churches' Response*, 80pp.

David Lochhead, *Shifting Realities: Information Technology and the Church*, 126pp.

Duncan Forrester, *The True Church and Morality: Reflections on Ecclesiology and Ethics*, 104pp.

Eva de Carvalho Chipenda, *The Visitor: An African Woman's Story of Travel and Discovery*, 96pp.

Gillian Paterson, *Love in a Time of AIDS: Women, Health and the Challenge of HIV*, 130pp.

Dafne Sabanes Plou, *Global Communication: Is There a Place for Human Dignity?*, 86pp.

S. Wesley Ariarajah, *Did I Betray the Gospel? The Letters of Paul and the Place of Women*, 72pp.